CAREERS WITHOUT COLLEGE®

OFFICE

by Shirley J. Longshore

Series developed by Peggy Schmidt

Peterson's
Princeton, New Jersey

A New Century Communications Book

Other titles in this series include:

CARS
COMPUTERS
EMERGENCIES
ENTERTAINMENT
FASHION
FITNESS
HEALTH CARE
KIDS
MUSIC
SPORTS
TRAVEL

Library of Congress Cataloging-in-Publication Data

Longshore, Shirley J.
Office / by Shirley J. Longshore.
p. cm.—(Careers without college)
ISBN 1-56079-353-8 (pbk.) : $7.95
1. Office practice—Vocational guidance—United States. 2. High school graduates—Employment—United States. I. Title. II. Series.
HF5547.5.L655 1994
651'.3—dc20 94-1860
CIP

Art direction: Linda Huber
Cover photo: Bryce Flynn Photography
Cover and interior design: Greg Wozney Design, Inc.
Composition: Book Publishing Enterprises, Inc.
Printed in the United States of America
10 9 8 7 6 5 4 3 2 1

Text photo credits
Color photo graphics: J. Gerard Smith Photography
Page xiv: © David Pollack, The Stock Market
Page 14: © Gabe Palmer, The Stock Market
Page 28: © Chris Jones, The Stock Market
Page 42: © Roy Morsch, The Stock Market
Page 56: © Michael Newman, Photo Edit

ABOUT THIS SERIES

Careers without College is designed to help those who don't have a four-year degree (and don't plan on getting one any time soon) find a career that fits their interests, talents and personality. It's for you if you're about to choose your career—or if you're planning to change careers and don't want to invest a lot of time or money in more education or training, at least not right at the start.

Some of the jobs featured do require an associate degree; others require only on-the-job training that may take a year, several months or only a few weeks. In today's world, with its increasingly competitive job market, you may want to eventually consider getting a two- or maybe a four-year college degree to move up in a field.

Each title in the series features five jobs in a particular industry or career area. Some of them are "ordinary," others are glamorous. The competition to get into certain featured occupations is intense; as a balance, we have selected jobs under the same career umbrella that are easier to enter. Some of the other job opportunities within each field will be featured in future titles in this series.

Careers without College has up-to-date information that comes from extensive interviews with experts in each field. The format of each book is designed for easy reading. Plus, each book gives you something unique: an insider look at the featured jobs through interviews with people who work in them now.

We invite your comments about the series, which will help us with future titles. Please send your correspondence to: Careers without College, c/o Peterson's Guides, Inc., P.O. Box 2123, Princeton, NJ 08543-2123.

Peggy Schmidt has written about education and careers for 20 years. She is author of Peterson's best-selling *The 90-Minute Resume.*

ACKNOWLEDGMENTS

Many thanks to the following people for their help:

Maripat Blankenheim, 9to5, Milwaukee, Wisconsin

Laura Boyce, Scott Paper Company, Philadelphia, Pennsylvania

Renee Campbell, Office Team Employment Agency, Minneapolis, Minnesota

Donald W. Cook, Director of Education, Academy of Learning, Mt. Laurel, New Jersey

Jerry Czenstuch, Dean of Admissions, Manor Junior College, Jenkintown, Pennsylvania

Conchita Delgado, Dean, Institute of Education, Future Secretaries Association, Stillwater, Oklahoma

Linda Gauldin Doggett, Professional Secretaries International, Kansas City, Missouri

Tara King, Merck & Co., Inc., Somerset, New Jersey

Motria Kramarczuk, American Red Cross, Washington, D.C.

Richard Melin, Marketing Director, Anoka-Hennepin Technical College, Anoka, Minnesota

Evelyn Miller, Excel Personnel, Philadelphia, Pennsylvania

Karen Nussbaum, Director, and Kim Fellner, Special Assistant, Women's Bureau, U.S. Department of Labor, Washington, D.C.

Carol Pam, Chairman, Department of Office Systems Technology, Middlesex County College, Edison, New Jersey

Caroline Rao, Berkeley College Placement, New York, New York

Diana Roose, 9to5, Cleveland, Ohio

Paul Savedow and Frank Bonifante, Workplace, Philadelphia Free Library, Philadelphia, Pennsylvania

Nancy Schuman, Career Blazers, New York, New York

Amy Soricelli, Katharine Gibbs School, New York, New York

Patricia Sutula, New Enterprise Associates, Baltimore, Maryland

Gwen Wells, Education Director, Office and Professional Employees International Union, New York, New York

Steven M. Wood, Director of Communications, National Association of Legal Secretaries (International), Tulsa, Oklahoma

Special thanks to Marian Betancourt, Jo-Ann Mahony, Dorothy Mandlin, Pam Rolle and Suzanne Savarese for their time and expertise, and to John P. Longshore for technical support.

WHAT'S IN THIS BOOK?

WHY THESE OFFICE CAREERS?

The administrative and clerical staff of a business—the people who are working nine to five (and then some)—are the spokes that make the office wheel go round. The jobs of office workers, who are the single largest occupational group in the United States, are undergoing great change. With ever more sophisticated computers, communications and transmission devices and software programs making their way into the smallest of businesses, the jobs of office workers are being constantly redefined.

This book focuses on five office-related careers:

- ❑ Receptionist
- ❑ Office assistant
- ❑ Bookkeeper
- ❑ Secretary
- ❑ Legal secretary

You don't need a college degree to get into these office careers. In several of them (secretary, legal secretary and bookkeeper), however, particular skills are necessary to get your foot in the door.

When hiring receptionists and office assistants (or clerks, as they're often called), employers look for candidates who are eager to please, quick to learn and able to deal pleasantly and competently with their co-workers, clients and bosses. It is the receptionist's job to greet visitors to the office, contact the person they are scheduled to meet with and direct them to the right department. Office assistants do a little bit of everything around the office, which might include operating the copy machine, running errands, distributing mail and making sure there's plenty of coffee.

Bookkeepers are the "behind-the-scenes" numbers people. Simply put, it's their job to account for money spent and earned. They record income (the amount a client pays for a product or service their company offers and when that amount is paid) and expenses (the amount and date of any purchase or payment made by the company to a third party or its own employees).

Secretary and legal secretary positions require strong keyboarding skills and a good working knowledge of the most common word processing programs. Strong grammar and language skills are a big plus in getting hired. Secretaries and legal secretaries spend much of their time doing clerical and administrative tasks. They type, correct punctuation and grammar and format written correspondence and documents that professionals in their office create. They make appointments, answer phones and callers' questions, keep files current and operate office equipment, among other responsibilities.

Those who are most successful in office jobs are effective at talking to and dealing with people, resourceful in solving problems, well organized and expert at making sure that things run smoothly. If, in addition, you have acquired several important office skills, you will find yourself in demand, since employers often want a person to function in more than one capacity—for example, as a secretary/receptionist or a bookkeeper/clerk.

In addition to up-to-date information about each of these office careers, each chapter includes interviews with people working in the field so you can gain insights into what it's really like. Before you begin reading the chapters, however, you may be inspired by the stories of three people whose office careers took off. Then find out what Ellen Bravo, the executive director of 9to5, National Association of Working Women, has to say about how you can make the most of an office career.

ELLEN BRAVO

on the Evolving World of Office Work

Ellen Bravo heads the organization 9to5, National Association of Working Women. Founded in 1973 by Boston office workers who were dissatisfied with their lack of rights and respect, the group now has 25 chapters. Its mission is to improve the status and working conditions of office workers through research, public education and activism.

For more than a decade, Bravo experienced first-hand the ups and downs of being an office worker. In 1982, she helped found the Milwaukee chapter of 9to5. In 1984, Wisconsin's governor appointed her an observer to the state's Comparable Worth Task Force. She is a spokesperson on many issues that concern office support staff, including pay equity, family leave and flexible work arrangements.

Bravo has served on state advisory councils and gives training sessions and workshops on such topics as automation, stress, sexual harassment and communication skills. The Wisconsin Women's Network voted her Stateswoman of the Year in 1989, and *Milwaukee* magazine named her one of its Giants of the Decade for the 80s. Bravo also served on the Commission on the Skills of the American Workforce and contributed to its report *America's Choice: High Skills or Low Wages.*

Bravo has not only "been there" herself but also understands very well the daily experiences of the 20 million office workers in America today. Here are her ideas about what the office of the future may hold for those who work in administrative support jobs and words of encouragement for those who hope to find office careers.

Working in an office can be a rich and varied experience. There are the other people with whom you work—a wide range of personalities, cultures and experiences. There is the challenge of being highly organized—figuring out the priorities, which tasks to do first, which ones can wait. There are the deadlines, the pressures, the conflicts, the new skills to learn, the old ones to hone and update.

Many employers want you to take the initiative and deal with multiple demands on your own, make decisions and proceed with minimal supervision. Office workers are often the first contact outsiders have with an organization, and the impression you make can determine the relationship they have with the company.

And the good news is that there are so many office jobs out there; the demand for qualified personnel is high!

In the more than ten years that I worked in office jobs in both large and small offices, I often liked the type of work I did very much. I typed very fast—and still do (100 words per minute). I took dictation from dozens of managers, all of whom had a different style. That was a big challenge at times! In some jobs I did a lot of writing and editing, which I particularly enjoyed. I also liked mastering new technology.

What I didn't like was the way I was treated in some jobs. At several companies, the policies—inflexible hours for support staff, for example—made no sense to me. I've always talked about office problems with my colleagues, who usually shared my reaction to working conditions that were not so wonderful.

The last job I had before starting the 9to5 chapter in Milwaukee was with a very large company. While I liked my duties, I felt that what I did was undervalued. How much work I got out was more important than its quality. And my employers were overzealous in checking it. That spurred me to want to take steps to help change the climate of the workplace, not only for myself but for the millions of women and men like me.

In the last decade, I believe that office workers have come to expect more for themselves and that employer attitudes have begun changing for the better, which makes the future even brighter for young people interested in working at office jobs.

Major technological changes have redefined how office support workers spend their time. Letters don't have to be retyped, only corrected on the screen. Pulling files to find a piece of information isn't necessary; your computer can do the searching for information in its memory in seconds.

Now there's more time for office support staff to use higher-level skills such as composing, editing and refining letters. If you have the interest and the motivation, you can learn some really interesting software and create better-looking reports and other publications like brochures and newsletters.

These days, receptionists don't just take messages, they "handle" calls, which means they use their judgment as to the urgency of the call, the information needed and who should get back to the caller. Secretaries don't just type a report; they help develop and complete it. An office assistant doesn't simply enter data in a database; she or he systematizes that information, organizing it according to the company's needs. A bookkeeper doesn't only enter the numbers in the right columns but utilizes a sophisticated spreadsheet program to help the accountants do their jobs better.

I took my first clerical job many years ago, as a secretary in the offices of a housing development, for the same reason as many young people entering the field now—I needed the income. I was expected to do very routine, repetitive tasks.

Now those in their first office job can often look forward to a greatly expanded set of responsibilities. Many companies are beginning to realize just how critical their office employees are to the smooth functioning of their firms. They are more likely to encourage and develop decision-making, listening, evaluation and problem-solving skills.

Involved workers are helping to create the future. I foresee a workplace where office support personnel can earn a series of certifications that verify their proficiency in different skill areas. On-the-job training will become more prevalent and more sophisticated, allowing office workers to learn new skills while performing their existing jobs. Managers say their offices cannot operate without their clerical staffs. I predict that the future will hold an upgrading of their jobs to reflect the skill those jobs require. There will be more opportunities for people entering the field to climb a new type of career ladder, aided by advancing technology and innovative company policies.

More and more, I see the words "clerical" and "career" going together, certainly to a greater extent than when I started out in the field. When 9to5 began, over 20 years ago, our slogan was "Raises, Not Roses," in an effort to begin educating employers to see that office workers were worth much more than a gesture on Secretaries Day. Later, we moved a step further to "Raises, Rights and Respect"—reasonable goals for a whole new generation of office workers who join the teams that keep American businesses up and running.

FAMOUS BEGINNINGS

Elizabeth Dole, President, American Red Cross, Washington, D.C.

Dole's first job was working as a secretary at the Harvard University Law School library. Thirty years and several degrees later, she was named U.S. Secretary of Labor, which enabled her to have a major impact on the workplace in which she got her start. During six presidential administrations, Dole served in several major policy posts, including commissioner of the Federal Trade Commission (at age 37) and U.S. Secretary of Transportation. She now oversees 30,000 Red Cross staff members and 1.5 million volunteers.

Estella Hernández Gillette, Deputy Director, Equal Opportunity Programs Office, NASA, Johnson Space Center, Houston, Texas

Gillette began her career working as a clerk stenographer. Her shorthand skill led to a job in NASA's engineering office. It's been straight up the NASA ladder ever since. She's held management positions in the national space organization's most visible areas, including the Astronaut Program. A problem-solver who welcomes challenges, Gillette received her college degree 22 years after she began her first job and her master's degree 8 years later, while continuing to work full time.

Lucie Salhany, Chairwoman, Fox Broadcasting, Los Angeles, California

In her first job, as a 19-year-old secretary at a Cleveland television station, Salhany was trained so well by her boss that she took over his job as the station's program manager at 24. She moved *The Oprah Winfrey Show* into national syndication while at Taft Broadcasting and directed the development of *Star Trek: The Next Generation* while working for Paramount. When she took her present position, Salhany became the first woman to head a U.S. broadcast network.

The reception area is the center of action in any office. As the person behind the desk, you can make all the difference—with your smile, tone of voice and helpfulness—in the first impression clients and callers form about your company. If you like hustle and bustle and can handle the stress of answering many phone lines, you may find that being a receptionist is the right office job for you.

Every office has its own pace: Some are hectic all day long, some have sporadic quiet periods and some are fairly calm all the time. Receptionists are responsible for creating a pleasant, businesslike atmosphere. Welcoming and directing visitors and answering the phone are their major responsibilities.

Being able to size people up and make good judgments is important; not everyone who shows up in a reception area belongs there. It's your job to buzz security or the appropriate manager if you detect something "off" about a particular visitor. No matter who you are dealing with, however, it's critical to behave in a calm, authoritative way without being off-putting. You must also maintain your cool no matter how many people, phone calls and requests are coming in all at once.

To be successful, you not only need a pleasant voice and personality but an ability to take down people's names, phone numbers and messages accurately. If you are working on a sophisticated phone system, you will need to master the controls—nothing puts callers off more quickly than being cut off by the receptionist.

Most receptionists are asked to handle some clerical duties as time permits. They often involve typing, preparing a mailing or inputting information on a computer.

The hardest aspect of being a receptionist is being confined to a desk for long periods of time. Until someone can relieve you, you usually cannot take a break because calls will go unanswered and visitors will be left to their own resources.

Performing this job well can give you a good reputation in the company and help you to learn a great deal about the business. If you prove yourself as a receptionist, chances are good you will be considered for other clerical openings in the office.

If you are a "people person" who gets satisfaction from giving out information and providing help, a job as a receptionist may be your entree into office work.

Getting into the Field

What You Need to Know

- ❑ Commonly used business words
- ❑ Basic office procedures

Necessary Skills

- ❑ Ability to quickly master electronic switchboards, multiline phone consoles or voice mail systems
- ❑ Ability to take accurate and legible messages
- ❑ Phone etiquette
- ❑ Ability to talk to and get along with a variety of people
- ❑ Ability to type 50 words per minute (minimum)
- ❑ Computer know-how a plus
- ❑ Office equipment know-how a plus

Do You Have What It Takes?

- ❑ Good listening and comprehension skills
- ❑ Ability to maintain composure even when others are rude
- ❑ Tolerance for answering similar questions over and over
- ❑ Ability to react calmly even when there are simultaneous demands for your attention
- ❑ Discipline to consistently arrive on time

Physical Requirements

- ❑ A pleasant phone voice
- ❑ A strong back (you'll be sitting in one place much of the day)
- ❑ A well-groomed appearance

Education

A high school diploma or equivalent is usually required.

Licenses Required

None

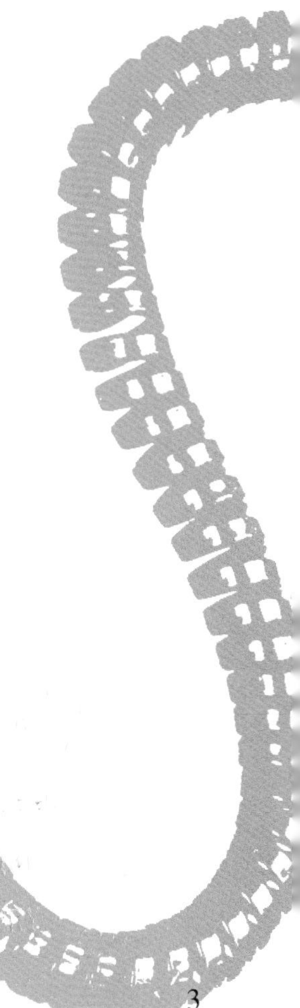

Job Outlook

Job openings will grow: faster than average

Turnover is high, and part-time and temporary opportunities are expected to increase.

The Ground Floor

Entry-level jobs: receptionist; receptionist/typist; receptionist/secretary; information clerk

On-the-Job Responsibilities

Beginners

- ❑ Answer phone lines and take messages
- ❑ Greet and direct visitors
- ❑ Give out information, handle customer requests
- ❑ Monitor security as directed
- ❑ Do light typing and other clerical tasks as needed
- ❑ Sort and distribute mail (smaller offices)
- ❑ Accept deliveries

Experienced Receptionists

All of the above, plus:

- ❑ Make travel arrangements for managers
- ❑ Handle busier or more sophisticated phone systems
- ❑ Conduct company business over the phone when appropriate (may do some ordering, handle more difficult queries, investigate a problem)
- ❑ Handle higher-level clerical tasks as needed

When You'll Work

A 40-hour-a-week schedule is typical.

Time Off

Receptionists receive the same vacation benefits (usually one or two weeks a year after working 12 months) as a full-time employee. Unlike some clerical staff, who may be needed to work on holidays or weekends when phones don't ring, receptionists are usually not tapped for this type of overtime. Sick days, personal days and major holidays are usually the same as those given to other company employees.

Perks

- ❑ Health insurance (most employers)
- ❑ Tuition reimbursement (some employers)

Who's Hiring

- ❑ Retailers and wholesalers
- ❑ Manufacturing firms
- ❑ Hospitals and health service companies
- ❑ Financial service firms (banks, insurance companies, brokerages)
- ❑ Schools and universities (public and private)
- ❑ Businesses of all kinds, large and small
- ❑ Social service organizations
- ❑ Local, state and government agencies

On-the-Job Hazards

- ❑ Back and shoulder strain (if your chair, desk height and monitor position are not adjusted properly)
- ❑ Stress-related symptoms (especially headaches) as a result of being "on" all day
- ❑ Hoarseness and other voice problems

Places You'll Go

Beginners and experienced receptionists: no potential for travel

Surroundings

Receptionists sit near the front door at a desk or console that is removed from the work space of other employees. The reception area is usually one of the most attractive and comfortable spaces in the office.

Dollars and Cents

Starting salary: $15,000-$17,000
More experienced: $22,500-$29,000
Part-time receptionists can earn $7 to $10 per hour. Pay scales tend to be higher in profit-seeking firms, especially larger corporations, and in major metropolitan areas.

Moving Up

Many secretaries, administrative assistants and experienced bookkeepers start out as receptionists. If you do your job well, try to learn as much as you can about the business on your own and let management know that you're interested in moving up, you will be considered for higher-level clerical jobs. If you take courses to improve your computer and other office skills, you will also be seen as someone who can be trained for more responsible jobs.

Where the Jobs Are

Receptionist positions can be found virtually everywhere, but the majority of jobs are concentrated in large metropolitan areas where many businesses are located. Approximately one in three receptionist jobs are in health facilities.

Training

Most training is on-the-job because each business has its own telephone communications system.

The Male/Female Equation

Receptionists are predominantly female.

Making Your Decision: What to Consider

The Bad News

- ❑ Confinement to one place
- ❑ Low pay
- ❑ Stress of answering many phone lines
- ❑ Having to maintain your cool when others don't
- ❑ Slow advancement and limited jobs in small companies

The Good News

- ❑ Plentiful jobs
- ❑ Regular office hours
- ❑ Opportunity to learn how a business works
- ❑ Part-time and temp jobs available
- ❑ Little training to get in

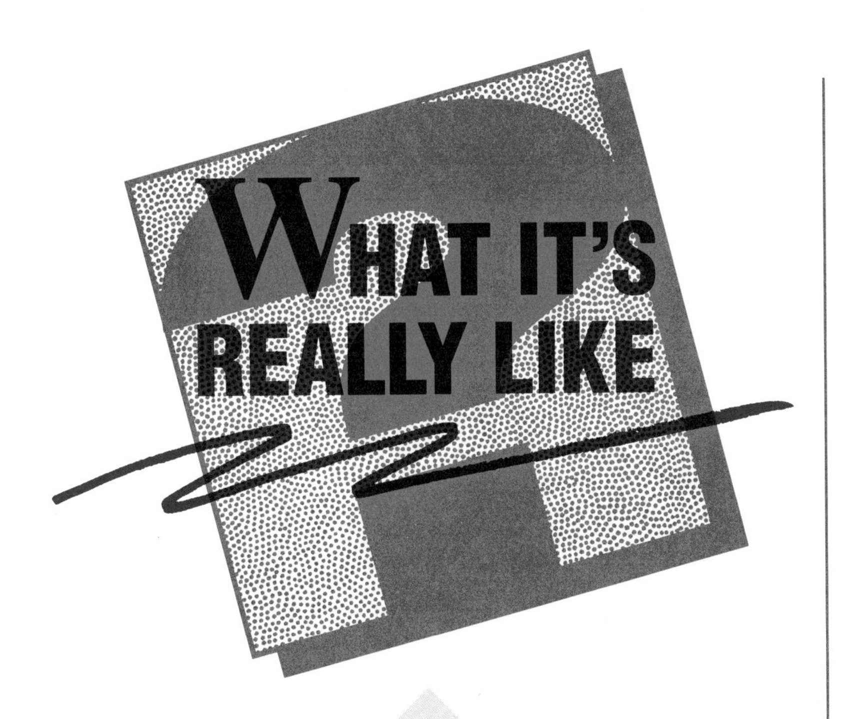

Robyn Levine, 25,
receptionist, Manchester, Inc.,
Philadelphia, Pennsylvania
Years in the field: six

What kind of preparation did you have for receptionist jobs?
In high school I took typing, accounting and basic business procedures courses.

Describe your first job and what you did in it.
I worked at the front desk at a video store chain. I answered the phones, helped customers and entered basic rental information in the computers. I got bored, so I was transferred into the inventory department.

Did you like doing that?
I discovered that I missed dealing with people, so I found a job at the front desk of a large casino hotel where my duties included making arrangements for people (setting up limousine transportation), handling 15 phone lines, putting information into the computer and taking in money. I did that for almost two years, and then I moved back to Philadelphia to take a job at a popular health club.

Was that job different from your first one?
Everything was computerized—all the scheduling for courts and leagues with game schedules. At first, the computers intimidated me, but I got intensive on-the-job training.

The phone system was easy to pick up, but I found it very challenging to take in money, get all the machines going and answer a million questions in the midst of a lot of activity.

What do you currently do?
I work at a job placement firm. I share the receptionist duties with another person—one of us works from 9:30 A.M. to 6 P.M. and the other from 7:30 A.M. to 4 P.M. Having a second person also makes it possible to leave the reception area for a few minutes when necessary. The phone is always ringing; when a call comes in from either an employer or a job seeker, I have to decide which counselor is the best match for the call.

We also receive resumes by fax, and I decide where each one should go. When people come to the office for appointments, I greet them and direct them and put them at ease. I do some typing, receive and sort the mail and help with bulk mailings.

Do you find the phone systems complicated?
Every system I've worked with has been different, but we have a voice mail system that transfers over, so I don't take that many messages by hand. I always give callers the option of recording their message or having me take it.

How long did it take you to feel established in your field?
I feel established now. I'm happy with my salary, and I feel that there is potential for me to move ahead.

What's the hardest aspect of your job?
Maintaining a pleasant attitude when I can have five lines ringing at once and up to 20 calls on hold. Most people are much easier to deal with if you are gracious. If I say "Please hold," I always wait for a "yes" before putting the person on hold. It could be an important client, and it could

mean money for the firm. I don't want to make anyone feel unhappy with how they have been treated when they call.

What do you like most about your work?
I like the people I work with. They appreciate my opinions and how I handle things, which is important to me. I enjoy greeting people and giving them a good impression of the company and our offices. And I like helping them out with their questions. I ask a lot of questions too, which helps me to learn more about the company and procedures. I might try to get more education in the future because I want to learn more new skills and my company has a tuition reimbursement plan.

What are you most proud of?
In the beginning I was nervous because not only were there the calls from the public but the inside calls from our 13 different offices. I knew it was important to recognize voices and names. I've been here less than a year, and I feel that I know people now and can be very efficient.

I am proud that people like me and appreciate how I do my job. I remember who someone is after only one call, and I go out of my way to track people down.

What advice would you give to someone considering this field?
This is a good job for a person who enjoys dealing with people. And if you push yourself to go further, you can.

Teri Jolicoeur, 25, receptionist, King Shipping Inc., New Brighton, Minnesota Years in the field: two

How did you break into the field?
I started at King as a data entry clerk. I worked in operations, filing and doing general administrative support tasks. When the receptionist quit, I moved into her job.

Describe your job and your responsibilities.
I cover 12 phone lines. The switchboard system was not difficult to learn, and soon we will be getting a voice mail system. I open and distribute the mail, type some letters and send out any mailings.

I am also responsible for accounts payable, which involves entering bills to be paid, going through my boss's notations on which ones to pay, preparing the checks and pulling invoices to make sure they match up with the checks.

What kind of preparation did you have?
I took the typical business courses in high school—typing, shorthand, accounting. I also took a one-year business curriculum course at a community college where I had intensive training in all of those skills as well as keyboarding, public speaking, word processing, administrative support and office procedures.

During high school I worked in a small office during the summer doing paperwork and answering the phone, so I had some feeling for the atmosphere in an office. I also worked part time while in school doing data entry, answering phones and filing.

Did you get any on-the-job training in your current job?
My employers showed me some things, but I mainly caught on to everything I needed to know by myself. That was fine because I like to learn independently.

What do you like most about your job?
I like talking on the phone and helping people. At first it was frustrating to have the phones ringing so much and to juggle the calls, but now I have gotten to know many of the regular callers. The office itself is a friendly and comfortable place to be. I also find entering the payables and handling the reports and checks interesting and challenging work.

What do you like least?
Trying to pay close attention to the bookkeeping when the phones are ringing all the time. It's also hard to be confined to a desk. I can't leave—if I step away to file, all the phones ring at once, it seems!

What are you most proud of?
I was given a word processing project to do on my own for a customer in Canada that was an important account. At first, it was a scary prospect; I didn't want to make any mistakes. But I took a deep breath and worked carefully. I was successful—the customer liked my work.

What advice would you give to someone considering this field?
You have to enjoy talking to people and smoothing ruffled feathers. I've noticed that if you have a congenial personality and are pleasant, you can calm down upset callers by the time they get connected to the person they've called.

Take all the computer and word processing courses offered. Take advantage of any training opportunities available. The more you know and can do, the better.

Sheila Clark, 39,
receptionist, The Calhoun School, New York, New York
Years in the field: 15

How did you break into the field?
My first job was with the Port Authority of New York, where I answered the phones and took messages. It was a small switchboard with about 20 lines. All of my jobs since then have involved taking care of the incoming phone lines, along with other administrative support duties.

What was hardest about your first few years working in this field?
At my first job, it was a one-woman operation and I was very intimidated by the lines lighting up continuously. I could never leave my seat, and there was constant pressure.

How many different jobs have you had in this field?
I left the reception area of Port Authority for a promotion to a scheduler's job at the airport. I conducted surveys, talked to people about their traveling habits and gathered information for the agency.

I then moved to a local government clerk's job, which involved a lot of clerical duties as well as answering telephones. During the eight years I was there, I learned how to use computers. After a break of several years at home to be with my child, I took a job as an office assistant in the financial aid department of Hunter College.

What do you do in your current job?
I sit at the front entrance of an independent elementary and high school of approximately 500 students. I greet everyone, field their questions and point them in the right direction.

I answer five telephone lines—seven if I am covering the admissions office. There are endless phone calls of every nature, from business matters to personal situations. This is my fourth year in the position, and I know all the kids and parents now, which means I can do my job much more effectively. I open and distribute the mail, accept packages and other deliveries. I handle all the school mailings, from folding and stuffing to addressing and postage metering.

What do you like most about your work?
This is a very endearing group of people to work with, and I love the personal contact I have with everyone. It's especially satisfying to help the students with arrangements they need to make and to know that they trust me. I like my role as a troubleshooter, and it is very gratifying now to have people routinely say, "If you want to know, ask Sheila."

What is your proudest accomplishment?
I've gained the confidence of my peers. The faculty and administration of the school respect my opinions. I am able to assist them in ways that are critical to the overall operation of the school. I feel that I am an important member of a team.

What advice would you give to someone thinking of going into this field?
To do this kind of job, you have to be extremely flexible. You should really think about your personality and whether it is suitable for so much interaction with people. You need to be a person who can remain cool and calm when it's

very hectic and people may be complaining and shouting instructions.

It's a job where you have to have a thick skin sometimes. People get offended at times if I don't put them right through or send them back to an office right away. You have to be skilled at being tactful, courteous and patient. Being a receptionist requires more skill than people think to do it right!

You may start off your day by sorting and delivering the mail. Then it's on to a mountain of paperwork that needs filing. Working as a clerk or assistant requires knowing how to do a little bit of everything. It's a great way to get your foot in the door of a company. To do well, you'll need an easygoing disposition and a knack for learning new tasks quickly.

Office assistants go by a number of titles, such as clerk or clerk combined with a function—for example, clerk/typist. Depending on the kind of company you work for, you may be expected to answer phones, type, file, do data entry (keyboard numbers or other information into a computer), run errands, operate office equipment or handle bookkeeping.

Experts predict a 24 percent increase in these types of jobs over the next decade, in part because office assistants are needed in virtually every industry. A wholesale show-room might need a clerk to greet clients and open boxes. In a real estate office, an office assistant may keep listings updated, field phone calls, direct customers to the right desk and check advertising copy.

In small companies, an assistant often handles all the clerical work. In a larger company, an office assistant could have much more specialized responsibilities, such as maintaining accurate and current data (a records clerk); looking up billing information, preparing invoices and seeing that they are mailed out (a billing clerk); or making sure that the company's documents are properly classified and indexed (a filing clerk). These tasks might be done manually or, increasingly often, on computers.

Being able to follow directions and get along with a variety of people are trademarks of talented office assistants. Many employers are willing to train you on the job if you make it clear that you're willing to learn.

This job is the kind of entry-level position that can take you places if you show initiative and get things done quickly and correctly. Knowing where to get answers to problems and showing good judgment are also critical to being promoted to a higher-level clerical position.

Success also depends on your technical skills—knowing how to operate different kinds of office equipment, from facsimile (fax) machines to copiers to phone consoles. Good keyboarding skills and a familiarity with word processing, spreadsheet, desktop publishing and database management programs will enable you to find a job more quickly—and move up.

If you're a flexible person who doesn't mind pitching in to get a job done, a position as an assistant or clerk might be just what you are looking for.

Getting into the Field

What You Need to Know

- ❑ Commonly used business words, including bookkeeping terms
- ❑ Basic office procedures
- ❑ Grammar and spelling

Necessary Skills

- ❑ Ability to use phone system, take accurate messages
- ❑ Typing speed of 50 words per minute (minimum)
- ❑ Knowledge of word processing and other commonly used office software programs
- ❑ Office equipment know-how

Do You Have What It Takes?

- ❑ Ability to talk to and get along with a variety of employees and customers
- ❑ Pleasant-sounding voice and good phone manners
- ❑ Ability to stay on top of details
- ❑ Willingness to do what's needed, when it's needed
- ❑ A "can do" attitude

Education

A high school diploma or equivalent is usually required.

Licenses Required

None

Job Outlook

Job openings will grow: about as fast as average

A demand for clerks in almost every industry, coupled with frequent turnover, will continue to create plentiful job openings. Part-time and temporary opportunities are expected to increase, and flexible hours are often available to clerks whose jobs can be done during nontraditional business hours.

The Ground Floor

Entry-level job: general office assistant, office clerk, clerk/typist

If you do a very specific kind of work, you might be called a billing clerk, a filing clerk or a records clerk.

On-the-Job Responsibilities

Beginners

- ❑ Do light typing
- ❑ Answer phones
- ❑ File papers and records
- ❑ Sort and distribute mail (smaller offices)
- ❑ Execute specific duties (a billing clerk, for example, writes and sends out invoices)
- ❑ Operate office machines (copying, fax, postage meter)
- ❑ Fill in for receptionist or others when necessary
- ❑ Run errands

Experienced Office Assistants

- ❑ Assume greater responsibility in area of specialization
- ❑ Supervise supply levels and order supplies
- ❑ Assist in overseeing maintenance and operation of office equipment
- ❑ Train and supervise beginners
- ❑ Handle more of the clerical work load (typing, data entry, file organization) as needed
- ❑ Set up and put systems in place to achieve smoother office operation

When You'll Work

A 40-hour week is typical, whether it's nine to five or eight to four. Depending on the nature of the business you work for (some are more deadline-intensive than others), overtime may be frequent or rare.

Time Off

After a year of full-time employment, you'll usually be given one to two weeks' vacation. The number of paid sick days, personal days and major holidays you'll get depends on the company.

Perks

- ❑ Health insurance (some employers)
- ❑ Payment for courses related to skill improvement (some employers)

Who's Hiring

- ❑ Accounting firms
- ❑ Retailers and wholesalers
- ❑ Manufacturing firms
- ❑ Hospitals and health service companies
- ❑ Financial service companies (banks, insurance companies, brokerage firms)
- ❑ Schools and universities (public and private)
- ❑ Businesses of all kinds, large and small
- ❑ Social service organizations
- ❑ Local, state and government agencies

On-the-Job Hazards

- ❑ Potential for eyestrain problems and headaches if main duties require steady typing at a computer terminal
- ❑ Back and shoulder strain (if chair, desk height and monitor position are not adjusted properly)
- ❑ Carpal tunnel syndrome (a wrist fatigue injury caused by repetitive keyboard motions)

Places You'll Go

Beginners and experienced office assistants: little or no potential for travel

Surroundings

Office environments vary enormously, depending on the industry and type of company. Corporate offices tend to be more spacious, well equipped and comfortable for employees. Many office assistants work in open rooms with rows of desks, or separated by shoulder-high partitions. If you have a number of responsibilities, however, you may not be as desk-bound as other office workers.

Dollars and Cents

Starting salary: $12,000 to $15,000
More experienced: $17,500 to $25,000
Businesses of all kinds pay more than social service organizations, state and local government agencies, schools and nonprofit organizations. Part-time office assistants can expect to earn between $7 and $10 per hour.

Moving Up

If you want to get promoted, you'll have to prove you can do your job and more. Volunteering to do tasks above and beyond what your job description requires, showing that you know how to solve problems and learning as much as you can about the work your organization does will all make you a good candidate for promotion.

In organizations where the office staff is sizable, you could move up by becoming more specialized in a particular function, such as bookkeeping, secretarial work or records management. If you have strong communication skills and demonstrate that you can train and supervise others, you may eventually be promoted into an office manager position—directing the efficient running of the office itself. Office assistants in specific clerking positions can move into higher-level secretarial or bookkeeping positions by improving their technological and communication skills and demonstrating competence.

Where the Jobs Are

Positions can be found virtually everywhere, but the majority of jobs are concentrated in large metropolitan areas where many businesses are located.

Training

Most training is on-the-job because each business has its own way of setting up its office systems. Most employers like you to have some training in office skills (typing, keyboarding, business machine operation) and procedures (clerical business practices, business math). Such courses are available in many high schools, postsecondary business institutes, two-year community colleges or continuing education programs at local high schools.

The Male/Female Equation

Most office assistants are women, but as office managers look for talented, all-purpose assistants with organizational skills to help run offices more efficiently, men may be more attracted to this field.

Making Your Decision: What to Consider

The Bad News

- ❑ Low pay
- ❑ Repetitive tasks
- ❑ Advancement can be slow

The Good News

- ❑ Jobs exist every where
- ❑ "Nine-to-five" hours
- ❑ Part-time, temporary and flextime opportunities available
- ❑ Little training needed

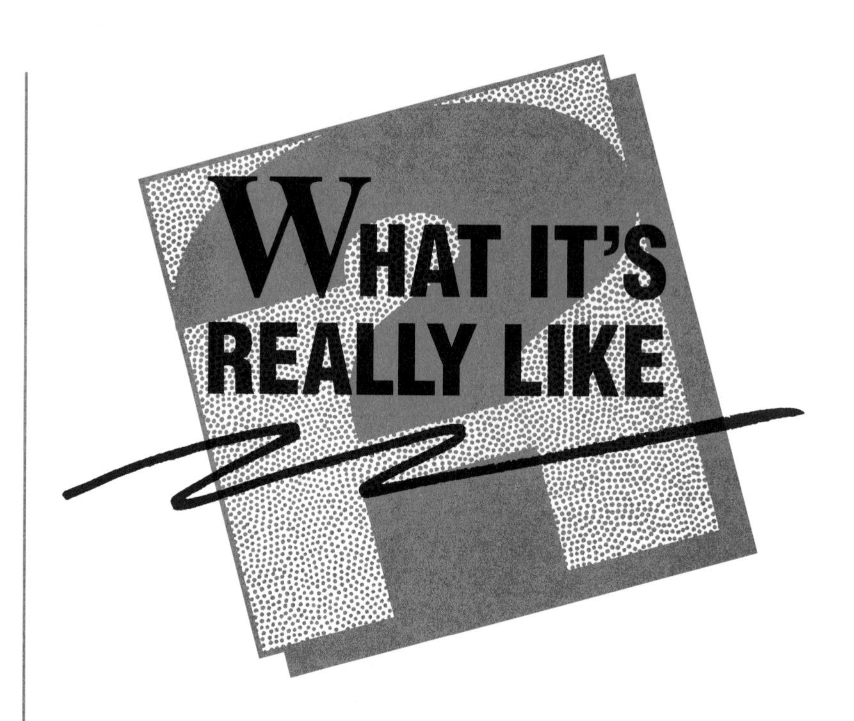

John Corniel, 20,
office clerk, New York Life
Insurance Company,
New York, New York
Years in the field: three

How did you break into the office field?
During high school I was in a co-op program at New York Life. It was a schedule that involved alternating working full time one week and going to school full time the next. I also worked here in the summer as an office assistant.

I gained a lot of confidence by working in a large office with all kinds of people. I also had to learn to organize my time and prioritize because my academic work load was the same as for students going to school every day.

What do you do on the job?
I process different types of insurance applications—pension, health, annuity and life insurance policies—up to 100 an hour. I am in the central records department, which manages the records of all policies. Each of us receives cards with the policyholder's name and number and the

application for a policy. I double-check the information, make sure the policy name and number are the same. I stamp the papers and manually file them in the proper places.

I don't have to do any typing, but I have to know how to retrieve data and enter it on a computer.

What do you like most about your work?
I enjoy processing the applications. I feel I'm participating in the flow of the company's business. I have learned a lot about the kinds of insurance people can buy and what the reasons are for purchasing them at different stages of life.

What do you like least?
I don't like filing correspondence. It must be done, and it's good exercise, going back and forth from my desk to the files, but I find it extremely tedious.

What are you proudest of?
My employers rely on me more as time goes by. They know that if they give me a certain task, I will get it done well. I feel that they have respect for me and for my skills, and that means I will move ahead. I also feel I'm making a contribution to the running of the organization.

What advice would you give to high school students interested in office work?
Computers are everything. You must introduce yourself to them and get as much instruction and experience on them as you can. You also must be patient in an entry-level job. You have to learn to relate to the people around you, who will be all ages and types, with different personalities. Communicating with your co-workers and bosses is essential to success.

Stefanie Jacobs, 18,
office assistant, Webster University,
St. Louis, Missouri
Years in the field: one

What prepared you for your current position?
I was the secretary to the athletic director at my high

school as part of a co-op program. I developed my organizational skills in that clerical job because I had to schedule so many things—games, transportation, rain dates—and I utilize these skills a lot in my current job. I am now the only administrative support for the director of the Center for Professional Development at the university. Taking care of all the details for seminar programs is one of my main responsibilities.

What are your other duties?
My boss teaches human resources to the personnel of big companies. She is gone most of the time, and I handle everything that needs to be done. I file correspondence, do word processing, write letters and memos from start to finish. My boss will tell me what should be said, and I compose and execute it.

I do data management, keeping our computer disks up-to-date. We do large mailings and follow-up letters, which I take care of. I mail out brochures and other requested information. When we are planning a seminar, usually several times a month, I make all the necessary phone calls and arrange the luncheon, from locating the restaurant to setting up the menu. I keep track of all the responses, run interference on whatever needs handling and figure out what to do when people show up unannounced.

What do you like most about your work?
Definitely the interaction with people. In this job I meet so many different, interesting people. It makes the work very exciting. The department hires experts to speak on various topics, and I handle the arrangements. I deal with training directors of companies and sometimes the vice presidents or presidents of the firms.

What kind of preparation did you have?
It has mainly been on-the-job. In high school I took every business course that was offered: four years of typing, information processing, computer applications, computer principles, accounting and office procedures.

As a member of the Future Secretaries Association, an organization for high school students, I coordinated a career conference. That not only gave me some of the skills I'm using now but it also opened my eyes to how many areas of business there are.

What are you most proud of in your career so far?
I am very proud of how I have helped pull seminars together. I'm the first contact with conference attendees. If they don't like me, or if I don't handle information well, they are not going to come. When something goes amiss, I have to make the arrangements to fix the situation.

What advice would you give to someone who is interested in working in an office?
Don't be closed-minded about any opportunities. Be prepared for anything that may come up in an office. It can lead to more responsibility and more recognition. You can't refuse to do things you are asked to do.

Being a team player is critical. If a job doesn't get done, it makes you look bad whether you consider it your job or not. You have to be willing to pitch in and to go that extra mile without feeling resentful and hostile. I work overtime often, but I see it as part of getting the job done.

Lorie Bower, 19,
office assistant, Canteen Corporation
Fort Wayne, Indiana
Years in the field: seven months

How did you break into the field?
After high school I took a one-year course at ITT Technical Institute on a scholarship and received an office technology diploma. Then I was hired to work for the assistant district manager at a branch office of a national vending machine company. My only prior job experience was as a crew leader and night manager for a fast-food restaurant.

Do you have a variety of duties as an office assistant?
There are only the two of us in the office all day—my boss and me—and I do all of the clerical tasks, from answering the phone to bookkeeping to handling mail and correspondence. I have learned to handle complaints and requests for

maintenance and information. The only thing I don't do is actually order the food for the machines.

When our salesmen come back from their routes every day, they hand all of their cash to me to tally, and because it's a lot of money, I count it in an isolated, secure room, alone.

What do you do in the course of a day?
I work from 7:30 A.M. to 4 P.M. answering the phone, and it rings all day long. I take messages and handle whatever comes up in the way of providing information on how to arrange for vending machines or servicing them. Every morning I review the route cards from our seven salesmen from the day before. I record the products they sold and add everything up to make sure the money that came in equals the sales. I do it manually, using an electronic calculator, and then I batch the cards and send them to the company's district center in Illinois, where everything is put on a computer.

I keep the cash logs in a ledger book, so I record the cash brought in and then put it on our computer daily. Some of the routes are on commission, so I figure the commissions out so that the weekly payroll will be accurate. Every week I send those figures to the head office in South Carolina, which is where our paychecks are issued.

What else do you do?
I fill out the purchase orders for the candy and food we put in our machines and figure out the unit costs for each bag of snacks. I also have correspondence or proposals to type. I file all the bills, invoices and purchase orders and order the office supplies.

What kind of training did you have?
In high school I took all the basic business courses—typing, computer literacy, accounting, shorthand and word processing. I also had an accounting lab where I learned Lotus and spreadsheet skills. At the technical institute, I built on these skills and also learned dBase, which added to my credentials when I was looking for a job.

What has been the hardest aspect of your first job?
I had to get used to the pace of an office and learn some of the specifics of this office very quickly. I had to learn how

to use the counting machine and the procedures involved in a week's time. My head was stuffed full of information, and I had to sort it all out so that I could set up a routine that would enable me to accomplish the tasks I was given to do. It took patience and a cool head so that I wouldn't get overwhelmed in the beginning. Now I have everything organized, and things are running smoothly on a day-to-day basis.

What do you like most about your work?
Dealing with people when they call. Most of the customers who call are pleasant and understanding if they need maintenance, and I explain that they have to be patient. I have only had one really angry complaint call to handle. I like feeling in charge of the office itself by doing everything necessary to assist in its daily operations.

What do you like least?
When I'm really cluttered with work and my boss interrupts me to find something for him. I've been in the job for such a short time, but I know where everything is. He's been here 35 years, and I'm teaching him how it all works!

I do get claustrophobic sometimes when I'm counting the money in the closed room. It's necessary for my own safety, but the isolation of it was something to get used to.

What are you most proud of?
When I first started this job, I had to learn all the computer programs in use here. It felt very good when I mastered WordPerfect 6.0 (a word processing program).

What advice would you offer to people considering this field?
Be very patient with the work. Learning the office procedures is important, and it can seem overwhelming at first. You have to check your work carefully and be accurate. You have to be aware of your grammar and spelling. Sometimes it seems like a lot to keep track of and a lot of pressure to do it right, but it's very vital to your success.

Bookkeepers are responsible for recording the numbers that reflect the organization's assets and liabilities, profits and losses and general economic health. You may think of a bookkeeper as someone wearing a green eyeshade and writing in a huge ledger book. But technology has changed the job tremendously. Today a bookkeeper's most important tool is usually a computer.

Bookkeepers (they're sometimes called accounting or auditing clerks) record and verify debits (money a company has paid out) and credits (money a company has earned), compare current and past balance sheets, summarize details of separate ledgers, prepare financial reports for managers and prepare different types of tax filings. They pay close attention to every financial transaction and post figures under the correct columns or appropriate headings, using a computer spreadsheet program or a ledger book (as some mom-and-pop businesses still do).

Computers have speeded up many of the more tedious and time-consuming tasks that used to be done manually. They can generate payroll statements as well as paychecks, tally monthly expenses and income to generate pre-tax information and churn out invoices, accounts receivable and payable and their age.

Despite computers, one thing hasn't changed since the Egyptian traders started keeping books in 3000 B.C.—accuracy is a must. If numbers aren't entered correctly into a calculator or a spreadsheet program, the computations won't be correct. To make it in this field, you must be good with details and have the patience to check and double-check your work.

Bookkeepers can be found in almost every type of business. One in three bookkeepers works for a wholesale concern or retail store. One in four works for organizations that provide business, health and educational and social services. About 25 percent of bookkeepers work on a part-time basis.

In large companies, bookkeepers may work in payroll, billing (accounts payable), receipts (accounts receivable) or another specialized area. In a smaller firm, you may be expected to perform office tasks, from answering phones to typing and mailing statements and collections of receivables, in addition to bookkeeping responsibilities.

Familiarity with computers and spreadsheet programs is a definite plus in looking for a first job, but many employers are willing to train a high school graduate who wants to learn the necessary skills and who shows an aptitude for math and number crunching.

If you're the type of person who finds satisfaction in balancing your checkbook and tracking your own income and expenses, bookkeeping may be just the job for you.

Getting into the Field

What You Need to Know

- ❑ Commonly used bookkeeping and business words
- ❑ Basic banking, billing and posting procedures

Necessary Skills

- ❑ Ability to do basic calculations
- ❑ Ability to use computers and learn new software programs
- ❑ Familiarity with spreadsheet and database software a plus
- ❑ Knowledge of the keyboard, particularly the numerical pad
- ❑ Ability to operate office equipment—electronic or manually operated calculator, typewriter, copy and facsimile (fax) machines

Do You Have What It Takes?

- ❑ Legible handwriting
- ❑ Strong powers of concentration and ability to be very detail-oriented
- ❑ Patience to sit for long hours at a ledger or computer terminal while you enter numbers
- ❑ Ability to perform repetitive tasks without getting too bored or frustrated
- ❑ Ability to get along with a variety of employees and customers, particularly in payroll, personnel and collections

Physical Requirements

- ❑ Good eyesight
- ❑ Strong back (to tolerate sitting for long periods)

Education

A high school diploma is required. Employers may give preference to those who have taken accounting, business math or office skills courses. On-the-job training is very common.

Licenses Required

None. A few states require bookkeepers who work on tax returns to be licensed.

Job Outlook

Job openings will grow: more slowly than average

Automation makes it possible for fewer people to handle bookkeeping tasks. But as the economy grows, there will be more financial transactions and a greater need for bookkeeping services. Most new jobs will be created in small, rapidly growing organizations. Part-time and temporary opportunities are expected to increase as more companies try to reduce their expenses by hiring bookkeepers during their busy times.

The Ground Floor

Entry-level jobs: general bookkeeper (at a small firm); bookkeeping, accounting or auditing clerk

Depending on your function, your title might be accounts receivable clerk, accounts payable clerk, invoicing systems operator, ledger clerk, inventory clerk, payroll clerk or billing clerk.

On-the-Job Responsibilities

Beginners

- ❑ Verify and record routine transactions ("posting")
- ❑ Make "journal entries" in ledgers
- ❑ Handle preliminary, periodic balancing of the books
- ❑ Execute procedures specific to your area of specialization
- ❑ Gather financial data for the accounting department
- ❑ Write checks
- ❑ Keep files in order
- ❑ Compute, type and mail bills and checks, make bank deposits
- ❑ Perform general office tasks on an as-needed basis

Experienced Bookkeepers

- ❑ Prepare trial balance, general ledger, sales ledger and aging of accounts receivable and payable
- ❑ Reconcile the general ledger (find and correct errors), bank statements, etc.
- ❑ Close out the books (make sure everything balances) at the end of a month or cycle
- ❑ Prepare financial statements
- ❑ Supervise other bookkeepers

When You'll Work

A 35- to 40-hour workweek is typical. Overtime may be required during busy seasons—the end of the fiscal year or quarterly or annual tax preparation time.

Time Off

Bookkeepers receive the same vacation benefits as other comparable employees at the company but are least likely to take days off during high-volume periods, such as the end of the fiscal year and tax preparation time, which can fall at any time throughout the year. Paid sick and personal days and major holidays are also given.

Perks

- ❑ Health insurance (some employers)
- ❑ Payment for courses related to skill improvement (some companies)

Who's Hiring

- ❑ Accounting firms
- ❑ Retailers and wholesalers
- ❑ Manufacturing firms
- ❑ Hospitals and health service companies
- ❑ Financial service companies (banks, insurance companies, brokerages)
- ❑ Schools and universities (public and private)
- ❑ Businesses of all kinds, large and small
- ❑ Social service organizations
- ❑ Local, state and government agencies

On-the-Job Hazards

- ❏ Back and shoulder strain (if chair, desk height and monitor position are not adjusted properly)
- ❏ Stress-related symptoms (especially headaches)
- ❏ Carpal tunnel syndrome (a wrist fatigue injury caused by repetitive keyboard motions)
- ❏ Eyestrain and headaches

Places You'll Go

Beginners and experienced bookkeepers: little or no potential for travel

Surroundings

The offices bookkeepers work in vary from tastefully designed, well-lighted environments to glass cubicles above a factory floor to windowless spaces. In a large corporation, you might have a small, private office or work at a desk in an open area with other office support personnel.

Dollars and Cents

Starting salary: $13,600 to $16,900
More experienced: $18,500 to $30,000

Part-time bookkeepers can expect to earn from $7 to $10 per hour. Pay scales tend to be higher in profit-making firms.

Moving Up

A high turnover rate allows good opportunities for promotion, particularly within larger companies. You can also move up by specializing in an area such as payroll, inventory or billing. Additional course work in accounting and financial software can make a big difference in how far you go. If you show that you're a quick study or take the initiative to learn additional office skills, you will have more opportunities within a company, particularly a small one.

Where the Jobs Are

Bookkeeping positions can be found virtually everywhere, but the majority of jobs are concentrated in large metropolitan areas where businesses are located.

Training

Most training is on-the-job because each business has its own way of setting up its financial records. Still, you may have an advantage over other applicants if you have taken high school courses in business math, clerical business practices, typing and keyboard skills and business machine operation. You can also gain skills by attending a postsecondary business institute, a two-year community college or a continuing education program offered by a high school.

The Male/Female Equation

Bookkeeping is dominated by women, but with computers playing an increasingly important role, men may be more attracted to this field.

Making Your Decision: What to Consider

The Bad News

- ❑ Having to bug people for payment (in collectibles)
- ❑ Repetitive tasks
- ❑ Being the bearer of bad news to internal management
- ❑ Continual pressure to do accurate work

The Good News

- ❑ Jobs exist everywhere
- ❑ "Nine-to-five" hours
- ❑ Part-time and temporary opportunities available
- ❑ Little training needed

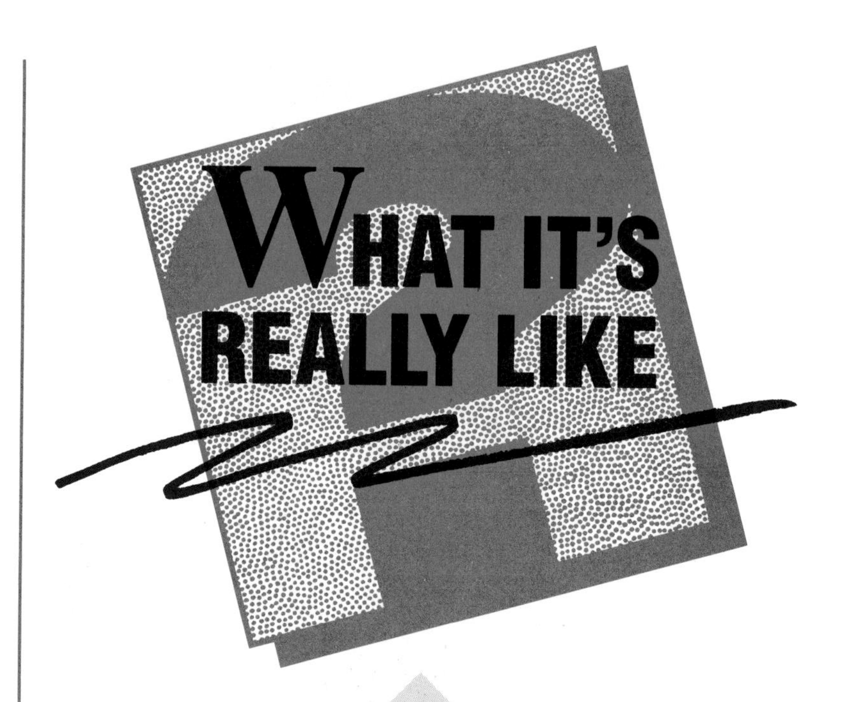

Melissa Stagnaro, 32,
assistant bookkeeper, Thermol Fusion, Inc.,
Hayward, California
Years in the field: ten

How did your career begin?
I had been working as a receptionist at Arthur Young, one of the "Big Eight" accounting firms, for a year when a bookkeeping position opened up. They offered it to me along with on-the-job training.

What did you do on that job?
I worked in accounts receivable doing expense and time reports. I matched up invoices and checks, which is very basic reconciling work. I was there for six years and received several promotions during that time.

Was your first job typical?
It was a good on-the-job training position because there were so many experienced people who showed me how to do things. In a small office, where I am now, you are more on your own.

What was the hardest aspect of your job at first?
Getting used to the variety of personalities I had to work

with. I was in an office with 200 accountants, and it was sometimes difficult to communicate with them because they tend to work with numbers in a different way.

How long did it take you to get established?
After about two years, I felt solid. But when I left Arthur Young and got into other aspects of bookkeeping, I realized that my knowledge was limited. At that point I worked at a variety of temporary jobs for two years. I got a feel for different companies and the people who worked at them, and I was able to determine what I liked doing best.

What do you currently do?
I work for a small firm that heat-treats metal. There are about 30 employees, and I handle the accounts receivable, which means I do all the credit memos and collections work. I do the billing, bank reconciliations and invoices and payroll. Because it's a small company, they need someone capable of answering phones and typing when needed. I am happy to do that because it makes my day more interesting and clears my head for some of my more challenging tasks.

What do you like most about your work?
I like the interaction and versatility of working in a small company. I also like collections work because there are interpersonal skills required. I like the challenge of "reading" people, being cordial while still doing my job—which is to get them to pay their bill.

What do you like least?
When billing is done incorrectly, because that makes my job harder. It makes customers angry; I have to go back and trace the information, and it makes me look like I have egg on my face when I go to collect the wrong amount.

What are you most proud of?
I really feel good when I can see the accounts receivable numbers go down because customers have paid their bills, showing that I have done my job well.

What advice would you offer someone who's thinking about entering the field?
Be sure you like numbers. You really have to enjoy working with them. If you like to work on your own and see the

calculations come out but you also like communicating with people, you can still be a bookkeeper by choosing certain areas of the field over others. Also, don't be intimidated by the technology. If you have a basic understanding of computers, you will do all right.

Caren Lee Savage, 29,
senior payroll specialist,
Cytec Industries,
West Paterson, New Jersey
Years in the field: nine

How did you break into the field?
One of my first jobs was in the personnel department of a large firm. I got on-the-job bookkeeping training in the payroll area. From there I went to another company where I developed personnel-payroll skills.

What did you do on your first job?
At that time there were no computers, and I did all the assigned tasks manually. I was filing, keeping time cards, entering payroll figures in the ledgers and doing some benefits work.

Was the position a typical first job?
Yes and no. When I started it was. I had dual responsibilities, being in the personnel-payroll area. But these two departments were split up, and I moved into the payroll end, so I learned more about figuring taxes and tasks specifically tied to being a payroll clerk. That prepared me for what I do now.

What does your current job entail?
I started here as a payroll clerk six years ago. I am now a senior payroll specialist. I still do filing and number input, but I have some more accounting types of tasks now. I still do journal and general ledger entries, but I'm also learning to do quarterly reports.

The department I work in has four people, and we all teach each other aspects of our individual jobs. It makes us all more versatile. I now do most of my work at a computer.

What kind of preparation did you have?
In high school I took a secretarial/office procedures course. I think that gave me an idea of what would be expected. I did temp jobs right out of high school for a while, and that gave me direct office experience.

What was the hardest aspect of the work in the beginning?
I've always liked numbers, but I found some of the more accounting-based procedures difficult.

How long did it take you to get established?
About two years. I had been doing only the payroll part, but the woman who was doing the other bookkeeping tasks left. So I had to learn very quickly and on my own to file state and local taxes and other more complicated tasks.

What do you like most about your work?
I like the numbers and I like the interaction with people, which is part of being involved in payroll. There are about 1,200 employees, so there are a lot of paychecks.

What do you like least?
When it gets tedious, which does happen every so often. I need new duties then! I need the challenge of learning how to do different things.

How does a person move up in this field?
If you start out in a particular area of bookkeeping, it's hard to make a switch into another area without starting all over and being trained again in those procedures, which are different. You can't just transfer from payroll to sales or marketing. It is smart to try to find out what the potential for advancement is in a company. My company, which is the business unit for a large chemical firm, is one that recognizes a good worker, and my effort has paid off in two promotions within my department over the last six years.

What are you most proud of?
The fact that everything runs smoothly in my department. We are very careful about our work because people's lives are involved. Employees want the right paycheck, and it's our responsibility to make sure that happens.

What advice would you offer someone who's thinking about entering the field?
You have to like numbers, that's for sure. If you try to understand what accounting does, it really helps, because you have to be able to deal with that staff's questions and concerns.

Lorri Hoyt, 33,
financial control administrator,
Scott Paper Company,
Philadelphia, Pennsylvania
Years in the field: five

How did you break into the field?
I worked in secretarial positions where I mainly did word processing. About five years ago, a bookkeeping position opened up in the corporate real estate division, and I applied for it. I liked working as a secretary, but I knew I had gone as high as I could go. Management was willing to let me give it a try.

Was it a usual first job in the bookkeeping field?
It wasn't a standard entry-level position because it had a wide range of responsibilities. I handled the daily transactions of the corporate real estate department. I billed out labor, processed invoices for payment, invoiced tenants, did the ledger maintenance for monthly closings and helped with financial plans by compiling anticipated expenses.

What was the hardest part at first?
I had to learn a lot, but fortunately I wasn't expected to know it all right away. For example, I had to become proficient in Lotus (a spreadsheet software program), which I only had minimal knowledge of.

What kind of preparation did you have for the job?
Typing and keyboarding expertise are critical, and I had that. The accounting courses I took in high school and in a postsecondary school gave me the terminology.

What do you currently do?
I'm now in the Worldwide Accounting division, which is much more project-oriented. We are responsible for the company's freight and distribution and book all the revenue for the company. I have a lot of autonomy as long as I get the work assigned to me done. In some areas I work closely with my direct supervisor; in others, with her superior. So I am learning a great deal.

What do you like most about your work?
The fact that there is a variety of tasks and that I have control over my work, to some extent. I have also had the opportunity in my current job to do some analysis, which is unusual without a higher level of education.

What do you like least?
Sometimes I receive unexpected requests for information that must be handled immediately, which is frustrating because I am not privy to why it's so urgent and I have to postpone other projects I'm working on.

What are you most proud of?
If I weren't recording sales figures, it wouldn't look very good for the company. My supervisors appreciated the fact that I turned last quarter's figures around so fast. They could then present that information to management for their decision-making process sooner.

Also, I got my associate degree in business administration a year and a half ago, which was paid for by my company's tuition reimbursement plan. It took me over five years and required great personal discipline to work every day and then go to school. But it was worth it.

What advice would you give someone who is thinking about going into bookkeeping?
It's a field where further education can help, but demonstrating both technical and personal skills goes a long way toward moving you up the ladder. You can show your boss what you are capable of just by persevering and doing the work competently, as well as being willing to do more than what you have to do.

Secretaries play a behind-the-scenes role in offices, but what a supporting role it is! As computer experts, they produce a department's written communications on word processing and desktop publishing programs. They often do number crunching on spreadsheets. They know where EVERYTHING is. Today their contributions are as critical as those of the professionals they work with.

In many firms, secretaries (or administrative or executive assistants, as they're often called) are expected to revise, edit and proofread their boss's written work for grammar, accuracy and content. Of course, they also produce the final document on a word processing, spreadsheet or desktop publishing program.

While getting written correspondence out is a major

responsibility for most secretaries, there are many other hats they must wear. Although many offices have automated voice mail systems that answer calls and take messages, secretaries remain the key link between their boss and the outside world. They have to decide which messages to pass on to their boss, which ones they can handle and which ones can be better handled by other departments.

In the course of an average day as a secretary, you will do everything from making and returning phone calls, relaying messages, sorting and opening mail, filing and keeping information up-to-date to word processing and data entry, making travel arrangements, setting up conference calls, keeping calendars current and making appointments, preparing expense reports and following through on earlier assignments.

There are many kinds of offices in every kind of industry, and every one of them has at least one secretary. So it's smart to choose a field—whether it's the arts, education, social service, health care or business—that particularly interests you.

Secretaries who become knowledgeable about their company's business as well as company policy and procedures often work independently and take on more complex responsibilities, such as working on special projects, coordinating departmental schedules, setting up conferences and seminars and drafting letters and memos.

The better your computer and software skills, the more indispensable you become. Successful secretaries also have excellent personal and communication skills: They're congenial, well-spoken, cooperative and tactful. If you're good at what you do, you can play a bigger role in the work of the organization and, if it's a large one, earn promotions and sizable raises.

So if you're willing to become a wizard on office software programs and like extensive contact with people, consider becoming a secretary.

Getting into the Field

What You Need to Know

- ❑ General business practices
- ❑ Basic office procedures

Necessary Skills

- ❑ Ability to learn and use office software programs
- ❑ Keyboard and typing skills (50 to 75 words per minute)
- ❑ Shorthand or fast longhand (to take dictation when needed)
- ❑ Good grammar, spelling, punctuation skills
- ❑ Office machine know-how

Do You Have What It Takes?

- ❑ Good organizational skills and ability to monitor details
- ❑ Good phone manner
- ❑ Ability to stay cool under pressure
- ❑ Legible handwriting
- ❑ Ability to work both independently and as part of a team
- ❑ Ability to use good judgment, keep information confidential
- ❑ Willingness to be interrupted mid-task
- ❑ Ability to talk to and get along with a variety of people

Physical Requirements

- ❑ Pleasant phone voice
- ❑ Strong back (you may spend much of your time sitting)
- ❑ No eye problems (you may spend much of your time staring at a computer terminal)

Education

High school diploma required. Business courses (including computer and keyboarding courses, office skills and procedures, typing and shorthand, business math and communications) are a plus.

Licenses Required

None. After six years of experience, a secretary may take a test to become a CPS (certified professional secretary) through the Professional Secretaries International association, which can open more employment doors and help in professional advancement.

Job Outlook

Job openings will grow: about as fast as average
The demand for secretaries—particularly skilled ones—is likely to remain strong. Opportunities for part-time (one in six secretaries works part time) and temporary secretaries are good. Some companies offer flex time (working the same number of hours but at less traditional times—7 a.m. to 3 p.m., for example) and job sharing, in which two secretaries perform the same duties on different days each week.

The Ground Floor

Entry-level job: Secretary (also administrative assistant or aide)

On-the-Job Responsibilities

Beginners

- ❑ Answer phones, direct calls, give information
- ❑ Take dictation and process drafts of written communications
- ❑ Keyboard or type correspondence, memos, reports
- ❑ Sort and file office documents, correspondence
- ❑ Proofread all written materials
- ❑ Schedule appointments; make travel arrangements
- ❑ Prepare expense reports

- ❑ Open and sort mail
- ❑ Operate office machines—fax documents, make copies, weigh and stamp mail
- ❑ Take care of boss's personal business (sometimes)

Experienced Secretaries

All of the above, plus:

- ❑ Handle special projects
- ❑ Draft correspondence, memos and reports
- ❑ Do research (by phone or in the library)
- ❑ Coordinate department activities
- ❑ Set up meetings, seminars, conferences

When You'll Work

A five-day week and an eight-hour day—whether it's nine to five or eight to four—are typical. At many firms, if you're asked to work overtime, you'll be paid extra.

Time Off

Secretaries receive the same vacation benefits (usually one or two weeks after one year of full-time employment) as other comparable employees at the company. Paid sick and personal days and major holidays are the norm.

Perks

- ❑ Health insurance (some companies)
- ❑ Payment for courses related to skill improvement (some companies)

Who's Hiring

- ❑ Retailers and wholesalers
- ❑ Manufacturing firms
- ❑ Hospitals and health service companies
- ❑ Financial service companies (banks, insurance companies, investment firms)
- ❑ Schools and universities (public and private)
- ❑ Businesses of all kinds, large and small (real estate, construction, transportation)
- ❑ Social service organizations
- ❑ Local, state and government agencies

On-the-Job Hazards

- ❑ Back and shoulder strain (if your chair, desk height and monitor position are not adjusted properly)
- ❑ Stress-related symptoms (especially headaches)
- ❑ Carpal tunnel syndrome (a wrist fatigue injury caused by repetitive keyboard motions)

Places You'll Go

Beginners and experienced secretaries: little or no potential for travel, especially if you are the one who "holds down the fort" when the boss is away on business trips.

Surroundings

Offices come in all shapes and sizes. The large offices of major corporations tend to be more elegantly decorated; offices in manufacturing plants might be located near production areas and are likely to be smaller and noisier. Secretaries usually have their own desk or work space, located adjacent to or near their boss's office. At some companies, secretaries sit at desks in one central area.

Dollars and Cents

Starting salary: $16,000 to $25,000
More experienced: $26,000 to $40,000+

Hourly rates for part-time secretaries range from $9 to $12, depending on skills and experience, location (urban pay scales tend to be higher, with the highest rates in the Northeast and California) and type of business. These factors also influence the salaries of full-time secretaries.

Moving Up

Competent, motivated secretaries who keep their skills current and who are willing to do more than is expected of them are in a good position to move into senior secretarial, supervisory, office management or executive secretary positions. Further training and education can help you move up, particularly if you take courses that broaden or increase your skills. Seniority and on-the-job performance also count.

Secretaries whose computer skills are superior are sometimes made information managers or chief information officers. Executive secretaries often assume some tasks that used to belong to middle managers—supervising other clerical workers, assessing information, taking on planning and decision-making responsibilities.

Where the Jobs Are

Job opportunities exist nationwide in every industry. There are more jobs to choose from in large metropolitan areas, where many organizations and businesses are located.

Training

High schools, business and secretarial schools and two-year community colleges offer a variety of courses and programs that can prepare you for a secretarial position.

The Male/Female Equation

Most secretaries are women, although the need for computer skills is attracting some men to this field.

Making Your Decision: What to Consider

The Bad News

- Inadequate recognition
- Low pay in some industries
- Repetitive tasks
- High stress level

The Good News

- Attractive salaries for highly skilled, experienced secretaries
- Opportunity to work independently (sometimes)
- Part-time, temporary, flextime opportunities
- Plentiful job options for skilled secretaries

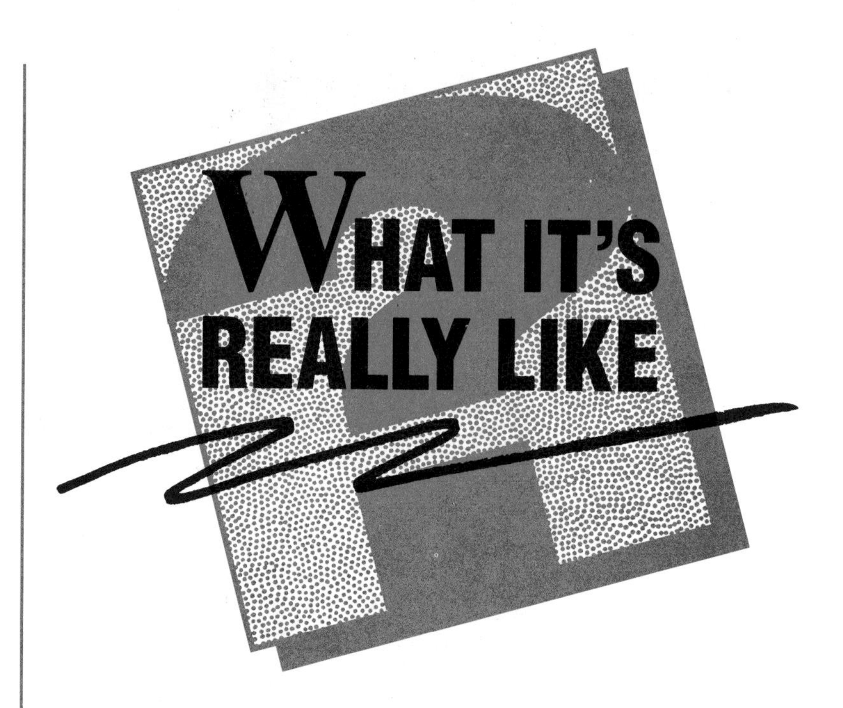

Judy Williams, 28,
executive assistant,
New Enterprise Associates,
Baltimore, Maryland
Years in the field: ten

How did you break into secretarial work?
I worked as a medical secretary after high school. I spent four years in the front office of a health maintenance organization, registering patients, keeping medical records up-to-date, taking dictation, typing, filing and answering the phones. I then became the office assistant for two psychologists, but I didn't like it because I was alone in the office a lot and I was used to being with people.

What is your current job?
For the last six years, I have worked at the Baltimore office of a venture capital firm with offices all over the country. I began as a receptionist, moved to an office assistant job and have been a secretary, with the title of executive assistant, for two and a half years.

What kind of preparation did you have?
In high school I took business law, accounting, office pro-

cedures and typing for three years. Each company has a different set of software and programs, but I was always able to pick them up as I went along.

What are your current job responsibilities?
I work for four partners in the firm. I type the board meeting notes from my bosses' notes and handle all correspondence. Many times there is a large mailing about a particular fund, which I handle. I make travel arrangements. There is also financial clerical work, since two of the partners I report to are the chief financial officer and controller. I keep track of the records of what is going in and what's going out and the cash flow forecasts, for which I use spreadsheet programs.

What was the hardest aspect of working as a secretary the first few years?
Knowing what people are going to expect of you and how to handle how they treat you. I learned not to take it personally if someone wasn't nice to me.

What do you like most about your work?
I enjoy being involved in a project, to learn more about the business our company is engaged in and to find out where our money is invested. It makes the work more interesting and makes me feel that I'm part of the team. I also like interacting with people, which I do a lot of in this job.

What do you like least about your work?
Days when the phone does not stop ringing. I cover all four bosses' phones, and some days it's hard to get anything done.

What are you most proud of so far in your career?
I started out as the receptionist for several general partners, and I have become their "right arm." They let me know that they have confidence in me. I set up important meetings and do other jobs that show me they trust my judgment. They listen to what I have to say and respect my opinions.

What advice would you give to people interested in secretarial work?
Look at the growth potential in a job. Try to find out if you can move up. If you aren't enjoying what you do and aren't

feeling challenged, it will be just a job. Also, stick with the tasks until you master them. In my current job, when I began typing numbers and financial information, I wasn't comfortable at first. The more you do it, the easier it becomes.

Mary Dykas, 27, administrative assistant, The Mariners' Museum, Newport News, Virginia Years in the field: eight

How did you break into secretarial work?
My first job was with an insurance group as a part-time receptionist/secretary, as part of a co-op program at the local technical college. At school I took courses in computers and advanced typing for a year and a half. I then got a full-time secretarial job with a spice company. I did a little bit of everything. From there I came to the museum, where I have been for six years.

What do you do in your current job?
My immediate supervisor heads up four departments, so I provide administrative support to 15 people. About 80 percent of my work is word processing—correspondence, memos and documents. I spend the rest of my time maintaining database files, updating information and pulling reports for review. I may create a table to help track an exhibit or develop and maintain master directories of information.

What skills do you find most essential?
Typing, of course! A good working knowledge of computers and different software used in the business world is essential. It's critical to be well organized also. You can learn technical skills, but if you cannot keep your desk in order and the files under control, and know where things are when someone needs them, you will have difficulty functioning well.

People skills are also required. You have to learn to "read" people and to get to know them on a business level. I work with many creative and well-educated people, and I've learned to pay attention to each one and be flexible so that I can handle the variety of demands and personal styles.

What was the hardest aspect of working in this field during your first few years in it?
It took me a while to gain confidence in myself and my abilities. It's hard starting a new job, and doubly hard when you have doubts. I would constantly ask myself if I was doing things fast enough and wonder was I asking too many questions. I expected myself to be perfect, but I know now that you can't expect it all to come together immediately.

What do you like most about your work?
The challenges and diversity of the job. There is something new every day, and no day is routine. Working in a museum setting is very interesting; I like the atmosphere.

What do you like least about your work?
Filing! I hate to file. Despite the presence of computers and databases, we'll never get away from having paper to file.

What are you most proud of so far in your career?
Recently I coordinated a telecommunications project with local schools. I was the information controller. I kept track of everything, worked with the networks, gathered questions and answers, coordinated people in all different locations. I enjoyed seeing such a major project through from start to finish.

What advice would you give to someone considering secretarial work?
Take as many business courses as you can in high school. I took typing all four years, so I kept perfecting my speed and accuracy. With good typing skills, you can transcribe quickly from tape and you will be fast at keyboarding. I also recommend taking as many English courses as possible. The more you understand word usage, spelling, grammar and punctuation skills, the more capable you will be. Read up on things in the world around you if you want to get ahead.

Cathleen Rauert, 31,
executive assistant, J. Crew,
New York, New York
Years in the field: ten

How did you break into the field?
My first job was working for the assistant general counsel at Prudential Bache. I functioned more as an office manager than as a secretary because I had additional secretarial school training after high school and I had secretarial experience from clerical jobs I'd done while I was in school.

In addition to performing secretarial tasks—typing correspondence, filing, logging in and keeping track of complaints—I supervised other secretaries. I scheduled vacations, arranged coverage for the reception desk and made sure all 30 lawyers in the department were covered with the clerical support they needed. I also helped get complaints assigned to the correct attorney.

How long did it take for you to feel established?
After two years I was promoted to the general counsel's office. He was also the Director of Corporate Services, which meant he coordinated everything from the employee dining room to compensation packages. We coordinated things between heads of departments—at one point I found myself choosing the colors for waiters' uniforms. My boss traveled a lot, so I made those arrangements. I felt very established in the profession at that point.

What kind of preparation did you have?
I took shorthand and typing in high school. The shorthand has come in very handy; so was learning how to use the Dictaphone.

In secretarial school there was a special, faster-track curriculum with courses that gave me specialized skills—a course in how to read the *Wall Street Journal* has helped me to be more astute in the business world. I also took marketing and accounting courses at a business college.

What was the hardest aspect of secretarial work at first?
Some people are condescending to secretaries, which is

hard to handle. I like what I do and I do it well, so now I can deal with this attitude better.

How many different jobs have you held?
I have worked in the main offices of major financial service, real estate, advertising, manufacturing and retail companies. The basic duties are similar, but I have done tasks I didn't expect to be part of the job when I took it.

Can you give an example?
I once worked as the secretary to the president and senior vice president of the custom event division of a large advertising agency. In addition to my secretarial duties, I planned major events—a Radio City Music Hall event for 700, a San Antonio tennis tournament for top executives and salespeople—which required great attention to detail, diplomacy and the ability to deal with high-level people.

What do you currently do?
I am the executive assistant to the vice chairman of a well-known retail clothing firm. I check sales figures and report on any relevant trade news every morning, schedule business meetings, make travel arrangements, keep all of the files up-to-date on the computer, handle correspondence.

I'm also a personal assistant to my boss; I buy and wrap gifts, make personal appointments and generally keep my boss's life organized. This frees her up to run the business. I usually work from eight A.M. to six P.M. or later.

What do you most like about your work?
I enjoy handling details; I like things busy.

What are you most proud of so far in your career?
That I've been able to reach a top level of my profession in ten years. When I go on an interview and employers see my background and experience, they want to hire me. That makes me feel very good about myself.

What advice would you give someone considering secretarial work?
It is really worthwhile and valuable work. It's gaining more prestige and is a career that is beginning to look better. If you're good at it, it's worth a shot because you can have a real impact—especially at the higher levels, where good support is vital.

Are you an *L.A. Law* fan? If you are fascinated by the law, you might want to consider becoming a legal secretary. You'll be asked to compile legal documents, organize case files and perhaps even deliver papers to the courthouse. You can be the right hand of a lawyer or judge who handles or hears cases that may involve criminal conduct or any number of other interesting legal issues.

The legal system could not function properly without skilled, competent legal secretaries who transcribe and type legal briefs (memorandums of points of fact or law having to do with a specific case), interrogatories (formal questions asked in writing) and other documents. Some also do legal research, observe and take notes during legal proceedings, file court documents and prepare papers such as deeds (a proof of ownership), affidavits (sworn testimony) and motions (an application made to the court for a ruling from a judge).

Opportunities for legal secretaries exist in many types of offices. Large firms and corporate legal departments are the most formal and most demanding of law offices; they also usually offer the highest salaries. You may start off as a junior legal secretary who is trained to follow in-house procedures and work as a floater secretary to cover when a regular secretary is absent. Government offices (local, state and federal court systems and agencies) usually pay lower hourly wages but offer more job stability and retirement plans. Small and medium-size firms are more informal and often offer flexible work arrangements.

There are also many types of law practices—corporate, litigation, real estate, wills and probate, criminal, patents, bankruptcy, family, personal injury, negligence and malpractice, public interest and environmental. Your own specialty as a legal secretary will mirror those of the lawyers you work for.

Although law offices vary in size and kind, they are serious and usually busy places to work. To be comfortable working in these environments, you should have a businesslike attitude, be willing to work hard and have the ability to remain calm under intense deadline and people pressure. It's essential to keep details of cases you work on confidential.

The volume of paperwork in the legal profession is very high, and much of your time will be spent doing word processing at the computer. Knowing how to transcribe from a Dictaphone or stenotype machine is very useful. Instead of dictating correspondence or reports, some lawyers use their own desktop computers to create drafts; secretaries must correct misspellings, punctuation errors and other mistakes.

Legal secretaries can move up to higher-level administrative duties, supervise other secretaries, become office managers or work for a senior partner or important judge. The potential for advancement is excellent, and good legal secretaries are in demand.

Getting into the Field

What You Need to Know

- ❑ Commonly used legal terms
- ❑ Basic legal procedures

Necessary Skills

- ❑ Ability to use one or more word processing programs
- ❑ Strong keyboarding and typing ability
- ❑ Ability to transcribe from dictation equipment
- ❑ Shorthand or fast longhand a plus (to take dictation)
- ❑ Knowledge of grammar, spelling and punctuation
- ❑ Office machine know-how
- ❑ Ability to use on-line legal or library references a plus

Do You Have What It Takes?

- ❑ Detail-oriented personality
- ❑ Stronger than average organizational skills
- ❑ Ability to keep information confidential
- ❑ Ability to project confidence and authority to clients
- ❑ Ability to be productive and calm under pressure
- ❑ Diplomacy in working with all types of people
- ❑ Ability to project a businesslike image

Education

A high school diploma is required. Graduates of legal secretarial training courses can often find their first jobs more easily than can those without experience or additional coursework.

Licenses Required

None. A legal secretary may take a test to become a CLS (certified legal secretary) or PLS (professional legal secretary) through the National Association of Legal Secretaries (International), which can help in professional advancement.

Job Outlook

Job openings will grow: faster than average

The demand for legal services is projected to remain high; so will the need for qualified legal secretaries. Part-time and temporary opportunities are expected to increase.

The Ground Floor

Entry-level jobs: junior legal secretary (at large firms), legal secretary, legal administrative assistant

On-the-Job Responsibilities

Beginners

- ❑ Answer phones, direct calls, give information
- ❑ Transcribe and type correspondence, memos, legal documents
- ❑ Sort and file papers, correspondence and documents
- ❑ Proofread and fact check
- ❑ Locate research materials in law library
- ❑ Schedule appointments
- ❑ Witness signatures on legal documents
- ❑ Fax and telecommunicate documents, make copies
- ❑ Prepare time sheets

Experienced Legal Secretaries

All of the above, plus:

- ❑ Do calendaring and docket management (keep track of court appearance dates and document deadlines)
- ❑ Proofread time sheets
- ❑ Work for a more senior-level attorney
- ❑ Manage the work flow of word processing staff
- ❑ Organize exhibits and documents during court proceedings
- ❑ Delegate work to other staff members or to outside services

When You'll Work

A 35- or 40-hour week is typical in the legal departments of many companies and in most court jobs. But expect longer hours (and overtime pay) when a legal deadline has to be met.

Time Off

After a year of regular employment, you can expect a week or two of vacation time. But if you work a lot of overtime, you may receive days off for "comp" time. Most law offices provide paid sick and personal days, but if you are one of only a few legal secretaries (or the only one) in a firm, you may be asked to come in on holidays if deadlines need to be met.

Perks

- ❑ Health insurance (most firms)

Who's Hiring

- ❑ Law firms large and small
- ❑ Legal departments of large businesses
- ❑ Municipal, state and federal court systems
- ❑ Local, state and federal government

On-the-Job Hazards

- ❑ Back and shoulder strain (if your chair, desk height and monitor position are not adjusted properly)
- ❑ Stress-related symptoms (especially headaches)
- ❑ Carpal tunnel syndrome (a wrist fatigue injury caused by repetitive keyboard motions)
- ❑ Eyestrain and headaches from staring at a computer screen

Places You'll Go

Beginners and experienced legal secretaries: little potential for travel

Experienced legal secretaries are sometimes asked to accompany their boss to court, which may involve travel to another U.S. city.

Surroundings

The offices of large law firms and corporations are usually tastefully decorated and equipped with state-of-the-art computers and office equipment. The decor and pleasantness of offices of small firms and solo practitioners depends on the financial success of the firm's partners and their interest in bankrolling attractive surroundings. The least attractive legal offices are those of the court system, government and nonprofit legal defense lawyers whose budgets are publicly controlled or whose mission is not to profit but to provide service.

Dollars and Cents

Starting salary: $20,000 to $27,000
More experienced: $30,000 to $50,000+

Part-time legal secretaries can expect to earn from $10 to $12 per hour, depending on experience, location (urban pay scales tend to be higher, with the highest in the Northeast and California) and type of law office (corporate and large law firms tend to pay best).

Moving Up

If you do a great job, you can expect to be rewarded with raises. If you work in a large law office environment, you may be able to work your way up to becoming a legal secretary for a partner or acquire office management skills. Or you may be promoted to manage the work flow of a particular practice group within a large law firm. Large law firms also offer you the possibility of lateral moves so that you can experience working in different areas of the law. The more you know about a type of law or office administration, the more indispensable you can make yourself, whether you work for a big or small firm. In addition to better pay, you may be able to take on lower-level tasks that junior associates or solo practitioners would do.

Where the Jobs Are

There are jobs wherever lawyers and court systems are found. The largest concentrations of lawyers are in New York City, Washington, D.C., Chicago, Philadelphia, Cleveland, Houston, Los Angeles, San Francisco and Boston.

Training

You can start by taking secretarial and business practices courses in high school. Most legal secretarial programs are offered by postsecondary business schools and community colleges. The National Association of Legal Secretaries (International) also offers correspondence courses and training courses through its local chapters.

The Male/Female Equation

Legal secretaries are predominantly female.

Making Your Decision: What to Consider

The Bad News

- ❑ Overtime often required
- ❑ Work pace and environment can be stressful
- ❑ Pressure to be fast and accurate

The Good News

- ❑ Strong demand for competent legal secretaries
- ❑ Higher salaries than non-specialized secretaries
- ❑ Part-time and temporary jobs available

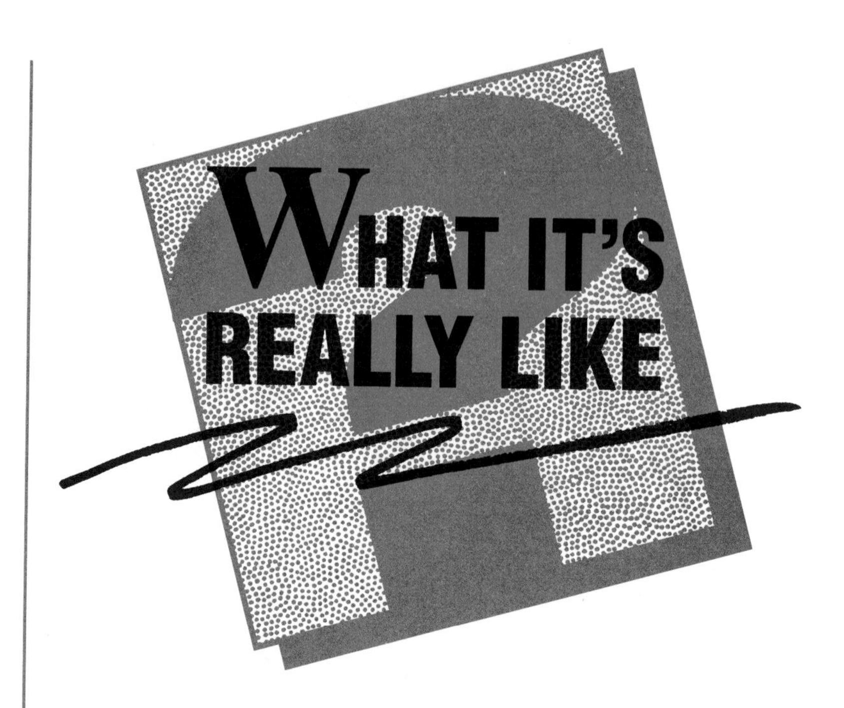

Timika Savage, 23,
legal secretary, Disciplinary Board of the
Supreme Court of Pennsylvania,
Philadelphia, Pennsylvania
Years in the field: three

How did you break into the field?
After graduating from high school, I took an eight-and-a-half-month secretarial/information processing program at Katharine Gibbs secretarial school. When I finished, I was proficient in typing, speed writing and business English and also in how to dress and speak for a good secretarial position.

My first job was as a "temp-to-perm" for a plant manager. After the plant closed, I learned of an opportunity to work for two attorneys. I talked them into hiring me based on my strong secretarial skills. I did all the general secretarial work and learned legal language and processes by working for them for a year. In that job I typed legal documents, did research, learned how to set up interrogatories and fielded questions.

Where did you go from there?
When the two attorneys split up, I landed a job in the legal department of United Way. Besides doing legal work, I also did charts and graphs and set up meetings and luncheons for a supervisor.

What do you do in your current job?
I process letters and complaints, do memos for lawyers and judges and do case management. After a case is documented and filed, I update the information when necessary and type the reports and whatever correspondence has to accompany them after investigators have done the legwork on a case.

What skills do you find most essential?
You have to be able to type or keyboard on the computer and transcribe from a Dictaphone. The lawyers are on the go so much that everything is on tape because they can't stop to write or even to sit down at their computers. You don't have to have formal Dictaphone training—you can teach yourself at home.

The material you deal with is also highly technical and requires that you be organized and detail-oriented. It's your responsibility to catch not just grammar and spelling errors but the content that might not be just right.

What was the hardest aspect of working in this field during your first few years in it?
All attorneys are not the same when it comes to deadlines. In my first job, I discovered that one of the lawyers allowed extra time; the other one didn't and was very difficult to deal with when he was under pressure. What I learned was that you can't take people's behavior under stress too personally.

What do you like most about your work?
Learning how the law works; hearing about cases, especially the human side of them. There's a lot of variety in my work; it's never monotonous to me.

What do you like least about your work?
I can have a really bad day if the pressure mounts and people are breathing down my neck. But you can't be a person who takes it home with you or you'll go nuts.

What advice would you give someone who is thinking about going into the field?
Don't let anyone discourage you. My parents wanted me to go to college, but I think I have done better by getting training and working my way up in the profession. In the legal field, you have to be sharp and have a mind for it. Since elementary school I have read newspapers and kept abreast of what's going on in the world. That's very important. It makes you more well-rounded and attractive to an employer.

Terry Flanagan, 25,
legal secretary/office manager,
Stamell, Tabacco & Schager,
New York, New York
Years in the field: seven

How did you break into the field?
When I was a senior in high school, I began working after school at the printing company where my sister was the office manager. The firm printed briefs for lawyers, and we also typed them if needed. I liked it, and after high school I got a job at a law firm with criminal, matrimonial and real estate attorneys. There, I worked for three attorneys and one paralegal.

Was it a "usual" first job?
It was fairly typical. I learned how a law office operates and what goes into preparing legal documents—there's research and legwork as well as drafting and formal typing, checking, proofreading and copying. I took materials to court and worked on legal papers like summonses, motions and interrogatories. I was there for two years before coming to the law firm where I am now.

What kind of preparation did you have?
The on-the-job training at my sister's office in high school was invaluable. I also took typing all four years of high school, majored in business and took courses in word processing and steno.

When I began at the firm where I am now, I worked for one partner and got on-the-job training that was terrific. He did a lot of drafting on his computer, and then he would help me finalize it. My predecessor taught me the basics of WordPerfect before she left, and I taught myself the rest. My boss taught me how to do research and make documents that were prepared for the court look right.

What do you currently do?
I work for a firm with three partners, three associates (all lawyers), one law clerk, two secretaries and a receptionist. The firm specializes in securities and antitrust law. I've been here five years and was recently made office manager. I supervise the receptionist and the law clerk. In this capacity, I have administrative responsibilities—billing (for which I learned a spreadsheet program on the computer), conferring with the accountant once a week, ordering supplies, managing the subtenants in our office suite and handling maintenance and personnel issues.

I work for a different partner now, and I am learning a lot about the insurance area, which is his specialty. He has recently become a litigator (a lawyer who goes to court) and is appreciative of my knowledge in that area.

What do you like most about your work?
I like fast-paced environments. There are things for me to do every minute of the day, so I don't get bored.

How long did it take you to get established?
It's been seven years since my first job, and I feel that I have moved up very well. I started here five years ago at $21,000, and since my promotion to office manager, which was the biggest salary leap I've had, my salary is $40,000. That, for my field and the limited experience I had when I was hired, is something I feel very good about. I feel that I demonstrated my competence and motivation and it paid off.

What advice would you give to someone who is thinking of going into this field?
You must have good secretarial skills and know legal terminology, which you can learn on-the-job. I have gone to one seminar on management techniques for my new position, but you learn more by doing the job.

Winston Henley, 38,
legal assistant, Lane Parker, Esq.,
San Francisco, California
Years in the field: nine

How did you break into the field?
After high school I worked for the phone company. When I decided to leave that job after six years, I took a job as a receptionist at a computer company because I was good on the phone. There was a computer terminal at my workstation, and I was encouraged to use the manuals and teach myself how to use it, which I did.

I wanted to advance, but there was no job for me there, so I left and worked as a temp. I was sent to a law firm, the third largest in the city, where I was eventually hired full time. I was already proficient on the computer, but they took the time to teach me legal terminology and procedures.

Describe your first job.
I prepared documents and proofread and managed them. I was responsible for all case-related documents and computer files and for knowing where each was located. These lawyers were working on multimillion-dollar projects in the corporate real estate division. Real estate deadlines can be killers; often I worked around 70 hours a week, sometimes seven days in a row. There was a lot of pressure.

Was it a "usual" first job?
For a large, prestigious corporate law firm, probably. Some jobs I've had since, particularly for private practitioners, can be more "nine to five" and less deadline-crisis oriented, but with many of the same kinds of tasks to perform.

What kind of preparation did you have?
I took typing classes in high school. There were very few males in the class. It is one of the most valuable skills I possess, and it enabled me to pick up keyboarding very quickly.

What was the hardest aspect of working in this field at first?
Learning the legalese; I didn't know what the lawyers were talking about at first. With on-the-job training, I mastered it. After that the biggest challenge was putting together the forms and documents that had to be processed.

How long did it take you to get established?
It took three to four years to feel that I had the skills to get the salary I wanted. I have worked in a number of jobs, and that has made me more diversified. You can earn more by moving around and not getting locked into a firm's salary scale.

What do you currently do?
I work in a two-person office now. I do everything that the attorney I work for doesn't have time to do. He is out of the office 30 to 40 percent of the time, and I am left on my own. I have great flexibility. My boss sets the priorities, but I have the responsibility of planning how they will be accomplished.

From 50 to 70 percent of my time is spent in word processing or other computer-related tasks: document preparation—drafting pleading papers for litigation—filling out form documents preapproved by the court, composing letters and getting them out. I spend one to two hours a day maintaining client files and making phone calls to the court and clients.

What do you like most about your work?
I like the responsibility of being in control of the office and having some say in how things are done. I no longer feel like just an employee. My contribution is important, and my boss acknowledges that.

I have to organize projects using my skills and creativity. In addition, I know that if I don't like where I am, I don't have to stay. I have found that legal secretaries can go anywhere in the country and get a job if their skills are good. And the pay is usually excellent.

What do you like least about your work?
There are some attorneys who can be very difficult to work for, and I have had to deal with stressful situations.

What achievement are you proudest of?
When I returned to San Francisco after working in New York for a year, I began working for a high-powered law firm, where I was part of a team that handled class-action suits against major corporations. It was a massive undertaking to organize, collate and put together 300 exhibits and boxes of documents. For several months I practically lived at the office, but when it was all over, I took my first trip to Europe on the overtime I earned.

What advice would you give someone thinking of going into this field?
Take advantage of opportunities. If employers are willing to train you, do it. You have to be willing to learn, work hard and know almost as much as the attorney knows, and in some areas—the format of documents, deadlines, filing procedures, court guidelines—you may know more.

MORE INFORMATION PLEASE

Commission on Recognition of Postsecondary
Accreditation (CORPA)
1 Dupont Circle, NW, Suite 305
Washington, DC 20036
202-452-1433

To find out if a business or secretarial school is accredited (has met certain curriculum, instructor and equipment criteria), call the number above.

Professional Secretaries International (PSI)
10502 NW Ambassador Drive
Kansas City, Missouri 64195-0404
816-891-6600

A worldwide organization that certifies experienced secretaries and provides information on the field to its members. Write for information on local chapters.

Future Secretaries Association

Chapters exist in high schools throughout the country. Ask your adviser for information or write to Professional Secretaries International (address above). The student organization, a division of PSI, sponsors seminars and conferences for those interested in entering the profession.

National Association of Legal Secretaries (International)
2250 East 73rd Street, Suite 550
Tulsa, Oklahoma 74136-6864
800-756-NALS (or 6257)

Membership in this professional organization gives legal secretaries information and the opportunity to be certified. Local chapters throughout the country have members who can help you with your questions about the profession. Write or call for information.

National Association of Executive Secretaries
900 South Washington Street, Suite G-13
Falls Church, Virginia 22046
703-237-8616

Call or write for career information or a referral to a member in your area who can answer your questions.

9to5, National Association of Working Women
614 Superior Avenue, NW
Cleveland, Ohio 44113-1387
216-566-9308

Write for membership information and a publications list.

WILL YOU FIT INTO THE OFFICE WORLD?

Before you sign up for a program of study or start to look for one of the jobs described in this book, it's smart to figure out whether that career will be a good fit given your background, skills and personality. There are several ways to do that, including:

❑ Talk to people who already work in that field. Find out what they like and don't like about their jobs, what kinds of people their employers hire and what their recommendations are about training. Ask them if there are any books or publications that would be helpful for you to read. Maybe you could even "shadow" the workers for a day as they go about their duties.

❑ Use a computer to help you identify career options. Some of the most widely used software programs are *Discover,* by the American College Testing Service; *SIGI Plus,* developed by the Educational Testing Service; and *Careers,* by Peterson's. Some public libraries make this career software available to library users at little or no cost. The career counseling or guidance office of your high school or local community college is another possibility.

❑ Take a vocational interest test. The most common are the Strong Interest Inventory and the Kuder

Occupational Interest Survey. High schools and colleges usually offer free testing to students and alumni at their guidance and career-planning offices. Many career counselors in private practice or at community job centers can also give the test and interpret the results.

- ❏ Talk to a career counselor. You can find one by asking friends and colleagues if they know of any good ones. Or contact the career information office of the adult education division of a local college. Its staff and workshop leaders often do one-on-one counseling. The job information services division of major libraries sometimes offers low- or no-cost counseling by appointment. Or check the Yellow Pages under the heading "Vocational Guidance."

But first, before you spend time, energy or money doing any of the above, take one or more of the following five quizzes (one for each career discussed in the book). The results can help you evaluate whether you have the basic traits and abilities that are important to success in that career. In short, are you cut out for it?

If a career as a receptionist interests you, take this quiz:

Read each statement below, then choose the number 0, 5 or 10. The rating scale below explains what each number means.

0 = Disagree
5 = Agree somewhat
10 = Strongly agree

___I have a pleasant voice and can speak clearly
___I have a helpful nature and enjoy giving people information
___I am a friendly person and have a congenial personality
___I have the patience to listen to people without getting impatient or irritated, even if they are rude
___I think I have the aptitude to quickly learn how different phone systems operate

___The idea of being in a visible and busy part of an office appeals to me
___I can handle sitting in one place most of the day
___My handwriting is legible and neat
___I don't get easily flustered and believe I can handle having several phones ringing at once
___I take pride in maintaining an attractive, well-groomed appearance

Now add up your score. ___Total points

If your total points are less than 50, you may want to reconsider your suitability for a career as a receptionist. If your total points are between 50 and 75, you may have what it takes to be a good receptionist, but you should do more investigation by talking with people in that job or perhaps even trying it on a temporary basis. If your total points are 75 or more, it's likely that you have the interest, motivation and personality traits to be a successful receptionist.

If a career as an office assistant interests you, take this quiz:

Read each statement below, then choose the number 0, 5 or 10. The rating scale below explains what each number means.

0 = Disagree
5 = Agree somewhat
10 = Strongly agree

___I think I would like doing a little bit of everything in an office
___I take direction well and can follow through on tasks
___I have a good telephone manner
___I am comfortable around computers and am confident I could learn how to use business software programs
___I can manage doing several different tasks at the same time without getting confused or forgetting details
___I don't mind running errands or even making coffee

___I can handle doing repetitive tasks without getting too bored or frustrated
___I am a flexible person and willing to help out in any way I can
___I get along well with many different types of people
___I'm resourceful when it comes to solving problems

Now add up your score. ___Total points

If you scored less than 50, chances are you are not cut out to work as an office assistant. If your total points were between 50 and 75, you may have what it takes to work effectively as a clerk, but be sure to find out more about the specifics of a particular job before you take it—responsibilities can vary from employer to employer. If you scored above 75 points, you probably will find success and satisfaction working as an office assistant.

If you are interested in a career as a bookkeeper, take this quiz:

Read each statement below, then choose the number 0, 5 or 10. The rating scale below explains what each number means.

0 = Disagree
5 = Agree somewhat
10 = Strongly agree

___Numbers fascinate me; I've always enjoyed math courses
___I am comfortable using calculators
___I feel that I could learn how to use spreadsheet and data management programs
___I can handle sitting in one place for most of the workday
___I can handle repetitive duties; I don't find them too tedious
___I am meticulous and patient with tasks that require close attention to detail
___I believe accuracy counts; I pride myself on it

___I am able to concentrate on a specific job for long periods without getting distracted or too tired

___I would get satisfaction from knowing that management relies on my work to make financial projections and decisions

___I enjoy the problem-solving aspect of making figures balance

Now add up your score. ___Total points

If your score added up to less than 50 points, you may not have enough interest or determination to become a bookkeeper. If your total points were between 50 and 75, you probably have what it takes to pursue a position as a bookkeeper, but you may want to investigate further by talking to people who do that job or by taking basic business courses. If you scored above 75 points, consider yourself a prime candidate for a job keeping the books.

If you are interested in a career as a secretary, take this quiz:

Read each statement below, then choose the number 0, 5 or 10. The rating scale below explains what each number means.

0 = Disagree
5 = Agree somewhat
10 = Strongly agree

___I have or feel I could learn keyboarding skills

___I know or feel I could learn word processing and other office software programs

___I am an extremely well organized person

___I have excellent command of the English language—spelling, punctuation and grammar

___I am good at following directions

___I am good at communicating information to others

___I get along well with all kinds of people—even those who are considered difficult

___I can usually stay calm and work effectively under pressure
___I have an upbeat attitude and a cheerful personality
___I'm not a person who has to get all the credit for a job well done

Now add up your score. ___Total points

If your score was less than 50, you probably would not enjoy secretarial work. If your points totaled between 50 and 75, secretarial work may be a good profession for you, but you might have to hone specific skills you will need to get hired. If you received a score over 75, you have what it takes to pursue a career as a secretary.

If a career as a legal secretary interests you, take this quiz:

Read each statement below, then choose the number 0, 5 or 10. The rating scale below explains what each number means.

0 = Disagree
5 = Agree somewhat
10 = Strongly agree

___The law interests me, and I'm not intimidated by the idea of learning legal terms and processes
___I don't mind spending hours keyboarding
___I am good at keeping confidential information to myself
___I wouldn't mind working overtime
___I can maintain a sense of humor and can work effectively under deadline pressure
___I am an extremely organized person and am able to keep details straight even when working on more than one thing at a time
___I can (or feel I could learn to) take dictation or transcribe from dictation equipment
___I have excellent command of the English language

___I can work for and with a variety of people, even those who are considered difficult

___I can project a very businesslike image in my dress and behavior

Now add up your score. ___Total points

If your total points are less than 50, you are probably not cut out for the demands of legal secretarial work. If your total points are between 50 and 75, you may have what it takes to be a good legal secretary, but you may need to increase your skills or look for a law office that offers you the work arrangements and type of boss you can function well with. If your total points are 75 or more, it's likely that you have the interest and motivation to be a successful legal secretary.

ABOUT THE AUTHOR

Shirley J. Longshore is a writer and editor whose articles about business, work and education have appeared in national publications including the *New York Times, Advertising Age, Ladies' Home Journal* and *Redbook*. She was a contributor to the book series *Career Choices*. A former editor of *Guideposts* and *Us* magazines, she now has her own firm, Writing Unlimited, which is based in Philadelphia and provides communications consulting and services to corporations, publishers and other writers.